PLANNED *Senior* MOMENTS

SCOTTSDALE

STEPHANIE RUSSELL, BSN, RN

Owner of Concierge Senior Care Management, LLC

Published by Stephanie Russell. (727) 385-9185. www.seniorcareofaz.com.

Printed in the United States of America

Table of Contents

Introduction

by Stephanie Russell

For anyone who's faced the challenges of a loved one's health scare or the daunting reality of managing an aging parent's needs, the feeling of helplessness is all too familiar. In the medical world, a seemingly minor health event can quickly spiral into a hospital stay, a stressful and costly experience for everyone involved. For seniors, these unnecessary hospitalizations often lead to a cascade of negative consequences, from increased risk of infection to loss of independence.

The good news? A different path is possible. Planned Senior Moments Scottsdale is your essential guide to navigating this crucial stage of life, offering a roadmap to help seniors age in place safely and avoid these unnecessary hospitalizations. This book is the first of its kind, born from a collaborative effort to highlight the dedicated businesses and compassionate professionals right here in Scottsdale who are committed to making this a reality.

Inside, you'll discover a wealth of local resources designed to help seniors and their families navigate the journey of aging in place. We introduce you to a wide range of professionals, from Real Estate agents specializing in senior transitions to Estate Sale companies that can help with downsizing. You'll find a curated list of trusted service providers, including private duty caregivers for daily support, reliable handyman services for home modifications, and experts who perform in-home assessments to identify potential risks.

For those needing more specialized assistance, we've included placement services, Medicare specialists, and professionals offering in-home tax and accounting solutions. We also connect you with vital support services like transportation services, hospice for end-of-life care, and companies offering home safety & security solutions to provide peace of mind.

Additionally, you'll learn about financial options like reverse mortgage solutions, as well as essential legal services such as estate planning and elder law services. We've also included practical help like home watch services for when you're away, and innovative health solutions like mobile IV services and lab solutions that bring care directly to your doorstep. By connecting you with this comprehensive network of professionals, our goal is to empower you with the knowledge and tools to ensure your loved ones can maintain their independence and quality of life, right where they belong—at home.

Planned Senior Moments in Scottsdale

Scottsdale is often celebrated for its sunshine, culture, and active lifestyle. It's a city where generations gather—parents, children, and grandparents—all seeking connection, stability, and the comfort of knowing their loved ones are safe and supported. Yet even in a community as vibrant as Scottsdale, families face the universal challenges of aging: planning for the future, navigating healthcare decisions, and making sure seniors have the resources they need to thrive.

That's where Planned Senior Moments Scottsdale comes in. This collaborative effort builds on the foundation of my first book, Planned Senior Moments, and brings the message closer to home. It's about giving Scottsdale families the tools and confidence to manage the aging journey with dignity, foresight, and a clear plan.

Why Planning Matters

Too often, families wait until a crisis occurs—an unexpected fall, a sudden hospitalization, or the realization that Mom or Dad is no longer safe at home. In those moments, emotions run high, options feel limited, and decisions are made out of urgency rather than clarity. Planning ahead creates the opposite experience. With the right conversations, resources, and support, families can navigate transitions smoothly, preserve independence as long as possible, and avoid unnecessary hospitalizations or premature placement.

In Scottsdale, the resources are here—but knowing how to access and coordinate them is the real challenge. From in-home assessments and concierge care management to placement services, transportation, hospice eligibility, and even financial assistance for low-income seniors, the options are plentiful. What's missing is the roadmap. Planned Senior Moments Scottsdale is designed to be that roadmap.

The Scottsdale Difference

Every city has its own culture, and Scottsdale is no exception. Families here often balance multiple responsibilities: careers, children, and aging parents—all while trying to enjoy the lifestyle this community offers. Seniors, too, may be independent and vibrant but reluctant to ask for help until it's absolutely necessary. That's why proactive planning is so vital here.

By tapping into Scottsdale's network of healthcare providers, senior living communities, local nonprofits, and specialized services like Concierge Senior Care Management, families can create customized solutions. Whether the goal is aging safely at home, finding the right community placement, or exploring programs like Veterans benefits and hospice eligibility, Scottsdale families have the support they need right in their backyard.

A Community Approach

Planned senior moments aren't just about logistics—they're about connection. Scottsdale thrives when neighbors, professionals, and families come together. This collaboration reflects that spirit, combining expertise from healthcare, senior services, and family support systems. Together, we can make sure that every senior in Scottsdale has the chance to live not just longer, but better.

Moving Forward

As you turn these pages, I encourage you to think about your own family—or the families you serve. Where are you today in the planning process? What conversations have you started, and which ones have you been avoiding? Whether you're preparing for your parents, your spouse, or even yourself, remember this: planned moments are powerful moments.

Scottsdale is more than a beautiful place to live. It's a community where seniors can thrive, where families can feel supported, and where planning today means peace of mind tomorrow.

Together, through this collaboration, we can ensure that Scottsdale becomes not just a destination for retirement, but a model for thoughtful, compassionate aging.

How Concierge Senior Care Management, LLC Can Help

Guiding Families Through Every Stage

Aging is never just about growing older—it's about navigating the choices, transitions, and sometimes difficult realities that come with it. Families often find themselves overwhelmed, unsure of where to begin, and pressured to make decisions under stress. That's where Concierge Senior Care Management (CSCM) steps in: to replace chaos with clarity, fear with confidence, and crisis with proactive planning.

At its heart, CSCM is about helping seniors age with dignity while giving families peace of mind. The services go far beyond simple care coordination. We provide a comprehensive in-home assessment, customized recommendations for referral resources, and placement services when remaining home is no longer safe or practical. Each piece of this approach is designed to prevent unnecessary hospitalizations, reduce stress for caregivers, and ensure seniors receive the right care at the right time.

In this chapter, I'll walk you through exactly what this process looks like and how it can transform the aging journey for families.

The Power of the In-Home Assessment

Every journey with CSCM begins with an in-home assessment. This is not a quick checklist or a surface-level evaluation—it is a holistic, detailed review of the senior's current health, living environment, daily routines, and support systems.

When I walk into a home, I'm not just looking at the person; I'm looking at the full picture. How are they managing medications? What's in the refrigerator? Are there tripping hazards in the living room? Do they have reliable transportation to medical appointments? How do they feel emotionally—lonely, anxious, content, or fearful?

This assessment covers several key areas:

Medical Review

- Current diagnoses and health conditions.
- Recent hospitalizations or emergency room visits.
- Medication management, including adherence and possible interactions.
- Upcoming medical needs (specialist visits, labs, therapy).

Functional Status

- Ability to perform activities of daily living (ADLs) such as bathing, dressing, toileting, and eating.
- Mobility and fall risk.
- Use of assistive devices such as walkers, wheelchairs, or grab bars.

Home Safety

- » Physical environment: stairs, clutter, lighting, flooring, and bathroom safety.
- » Emergency preparedness: working smoke detectors, emergency contacts, accessibility of phones.
- » Modifications needed for long-term safety (grab bars, ramps, shower chairs, railings).

Social and Emotional Well-Being

- » Current support network: family, friends, caregivers, neighbors.
- » Community involvement and socialization opportunities.
- » Risks of isolation, depression, or cognitive decline.

Financial and Legal Considerations

- » Eligibility for community programs, veterans' benefits, or Medicaid assistance.
- » Existing advanced directives or power of attorney documents.
- » Ability to afford in-home care, senior housing, or medical services.

This comprehensive picture allows me to see not only what is happening now, but what could happen if certain risks aren't addressed. For example, I may find that a client's cluttered living room and use of multiple medications create a perfect storm for a fall and hospitalization. Or I might see that a client has no transportation, which means they are likely to miss critical doctor visits.

The in-home assessment isn't just data collection—it's about building trust. Seniors and families often feel overwhelmed, but when someone takes the time to listen, observe, and truly understand their situation, they feel heard and supported. That trust is the foundation for everything that comes next.

Recommendations for Aging in Place Safely

Once the in-home assessment is complete, the next step is creating a personalized care plan. This plan outlines specific recommendations, tailored resources, and referrals to support the senior's ability to age safely at home.

Here's how this stage works:

Medical Coordination

I identify gaps in medical care and connect clients with appropriate professionals:

- **Primary Care & Specialists:** Ensuring seniors have a strong medical team who communicates effectively.
- **Home Health Services:** Skilled nursing, physical therapy, and occupational therapy for post-hospital recovery or chronic condition management.
- **Medication Management:** Referrals to pharmacists or programs that help with blister packs, medication reminders, and safe administration.

Home Safety Enhancements

Through partnerships with home modification companies and occupational therapists, we arrange for:

- Grab bar installation.
- Non-slip flooring.
- Improved lighting.
- Stair lifts or ramp systems.
- Emergency response systems.

These changes are often small but have an enormous impact on preventing falls and keeping seniors independent.

Support Services

Referrals may include:

- **Transportation:** Ride programs, senior shuttles, or vetted private drivers.
- **Meals:** Meal delivery services or community dining programs.
- **Companion Care:** Trained caregivers who provide help with errands, personal care, or companionship.
- **Social Engagement:** Day programs, senior centers, or faith-based community groups.

Financial and Legal Guidance

We connect families with resources such as:

- Veteran's Aid & Attendance benefits.
- Medicaid planning assistance.
- Long-term care insurance navigation.

» Elder law attorneys for wills, trusts, and guardianship needs.

The goal is to make the home not only safer, but also more sustainable for long-term living. The truth is, most seniors want to stay in their homes for as long as possible. By addressing risks and connecting them with the right resources, we make that dream a reality—while also sparing families the stress and financial burden of frequent hospital visits.

Preventing Unnecessary Hospitalizations

One of the greatest benefits of concierge senior care management is the prevention of hospitalizations. Hospital stays for seniors are not just expensive—they can also be traumatic. A single hospitalization can lead to a loss of independence, cognitive decline, or long-term complications.

Through early intervention and continuous monitoring, CSCM helps families avoid these crises. Here's how:

- **Care Transition Coaching:** After a hospital or rehab discharge, we help seniors understand discharge instructions, fill medications, and attend follow-up appointments. This alone drastically reduces readmissions.
- **Early Warning Signs:** Families are educated on what symptoms to watch for and when to call for help—catching problems before they spiral into emergencies.
- **Coordination with Providers:** We maintain direct communication with doctors, therapists, and home health nurses, ensuring no one falls through the cracks.

This proactive approach changes the entire healthcare experience. Instead of the cycle of "hospital—home—rehospitalization," families can stabilize their loved ones and focus on quality of life.

Placement Services: When Home is No Longer an Option

As much as we advocate for aging in place, there are times when remaining at home is no longer safe or feasible. This realization is often painful for families, but with the right guidance, it doesn't have to be overwhelming.

Placement services are the next phase of CSCM. They begin with the same compassionate, individualized approach:

Step 1: Understanding the Senior's Needs

We assess not only medical and functional requirements, but also emotional, spiritual, and lifestyle preferences. Does the senior want a community with active social opportunities? Do they need memory care? Do they prefer a smaller, homelike setting or a larger community with robust amenities?

Step 2: Matching with Communities

We curate a shortlist of senior living communities—assisted living, memory care, group homes, or skilled nursing facilities—that fit the senior's needs and budget. Importantly, these referrals are unbiased. Families can trust that recommendations are based on the client's best interest, not financial incentives.

Step 3:
Tours and Transitions

We accompany families on tours, ask the tough questions they may not think of, and help compare options. Once a decision is made, we coordinate the move, communicate with the new care team, and ensure a smooth transition.

Step 4:
Ongoing Support

Even after placement, CSCM remains involved to monitor satisfaction and care quality. Families know they are not alone—they have an advocate who continues to check in.

The placement process is not just about finding a bed. It's about finding the right environment where a senior can feel safe, supported, and valued. Done well, it brings relief to families and restores dignity to the senior.

The Human Side of Care Management

While the processes and services are critical, what truly defines CSCM is the human side. Families often tell me that the most valuable thing we provide isn't just resources—it's reassurance.

They no longer feel like they are navigating a maze on their own. Instead, they have a guide who understands both the medical system and the emotional realities of aging. They feel empowered to make informed decisions rather than pressured into hasty ones.

One family described it perfectly: "You gave us back control during a time we felt like we had none."

That's the heart of concierge senior care management.

Conclusion: A Roadmap for Aging Well

Aging is inevitable, but suffering through it unnecessarily is not. With an in-home assessment, carefully tailored recommendations, and placement services when needed, families can replace fear with foresight.

Concierge Senior Care Management offers exactly that—a roadmap that guides seniors and families through every stage. From preventing falls and hospitalizations at home to making thoughtful transitions into care communities, CSCM ensures that no one has to face the journey alone.

The truth is, we can't always control the challenges of aging. But with the right planning, resources, and support, we can control how we respond to them. And that makes all the difference—for seniors, for families, and for the Scottsdale community we serve.

Stephanie's Special Offer

Navigating senior care can be overwhelming. We're here to help. Reach out today for dedicated support and a seamless care experience for your family. Call at 480-679-4219 or visit CSCM www.seniorcareofaz.com/contact

Innovations in Elderly Care:

The Power of Hydration and Wellness

by Angela Garrett

The Aging Process and its Challenges

Aging is a journey accompanied by various physiological changes that can dramatically affect an individual's overall health and well-being. As the human body evolves with age, maintaining vital functions becomes increasingly paramount, necessitating adaptations in lifestyle and healthcare approaches tailored specifically to the elderly.

The importance of hydration often remains underestimated among the elderly, and yet its role in health and vitality cannot be overstated. Dehydration poses a serious threat due to its potential to cause numerous health complications that can impair the quality of life for older adults. Understanding and addressing these hydration challenges is crucial for enhancing the well-being of the elderly population.

The Silent Epidemic: Dehydration in Older Adults

As the body ages, its composition and functionality shift, making hydration critical to proper operation. With the human body composed of roughly 60 percent water, sustaining this balance is essential for vitality. Unfortunately, the elderly often experience a diminished thirst sensation, contributing to inadequate fluid intake. This decrease in thirst sensitivity, coupled with factors such as medications that act as diuretics and reduced kidney function, escalates the risk of dehydration significantly.

Dehydration can lead to a range of serious health issues among the elderly, including urinary tract infections, kidney stones, chronic constipation, cognitive decline, and an increased risk of falls due to dizziness and muscle weakness. Therefore, it's not merely about quenching thirst but ensuring that the body has sufficient fluids to uphold critical functions—particularly in a demographic more susceptible to these adverse effects.

Prime IV Hydration and Wellness: Innovating Care with Mobile IV Services

Our company, Prime IV Hydration and Wellness, recognizes the gravity of hydration in elderly care, launching mobile IV services specifically tailored for older adults. By partnering with various senior living facilities across the Valley, Prime IV delivers innovative hydration solutions directly to those age fifty and older. This initiative acts as a lifeline, addressing unique hydration needs with customized therapies designed to boost health and vitality.

IV hydration therapy has emerged as a remarkably effective method to tackle dehydration among the elderly. Unlike traditional oral hydration strategies, IV therapy facilitates the rapid delivery of fluids directly into the bloodstream, ensuring immediate absorption and rehydration. This approach is particularly beneficial for individuals who may face challenges in consuming large water volumes due to physical limitations or conditions affecting nutrient absorption.

The Multifaceted Benefits of Hydration

Hydration extends beyond merely satiating thirst; it plays a vital role in overall health management. For older adults, staying adequately hydrated is crucial for several reasons:

- **Cognitive Function:** Proper hydration can prevent the exacerbation of dementia symptoms and other cognitive impairments.
- **Medication Efficacy:** Water aids in the absorption and effectiveness of various medications, preventing adverse reactions and ensuring optimal functionality.
- **Electrolyte Balance:** Maintaining adequate hydration safeguards against electrolyte imbalances that can be life-threatening.
- **Physical Health:** Hydration helps regulate body temperature, supports healthy skin, improves digestion, and reduces the risk of falls by maintaining muscle function.

Building a Community of Care: Expanding Beyond Services

Prime IV's approach is not only about service provision, but also about fostering a supportive community around its elderly clientele. By collaborating with senior living facilities and communities, a network of care is established that prioritizes the health and well-being of older adults, ensuring they receive necessary fluids and nutrients to manage chronic conditions and mitigate the risk of serious health issues.

Seasonal Wellness Practices: Embracing the Change in Seasons

As seasons transition, many individuals, including the elderly, face changes in energy and hydration levels. The dry air of winter can exacerbate fatigue and dehydration, making spring the ideal time to refresh, recharge, and adopt healthier habits. IV therapy is particularly beneficial during seasonal changes, delivering hydration, vitamins, and antioxidants directly into the bloodstream for fast and efficient absorption. This practice supports an array of wellness goals, from boosting energy and enhancing immune function to promoting healthy, glowing skin.

Comprehensive Wellness Goals and Therapies

Prime IV's initiatives align with broader wellness objectives, harnessing the capabilities of IV therapy to support detoxification, radiant skin, recovery, stress management, and immune strength among its elderly patients. Targeting these specific areas through tailored therapies helps older adults combat stress, stay active, and fully engage with their personal wellness goals. Innovative IV therapies offer a range of benefits:

- **Detox and Reset:** Antioxidants in IV treatments help eliminate toxins, invigorating metabolism and leaving individuals feeling more energized.
- **Radiant Skin:** By supporting collagen production, IV hydration promotes hydrated skin and stronger hair and nails, contributing to a natural glow.
- **Recovery Support:** Essential nutrients in IV therapy enhance physical performance, reduce muscle soreness, and accelerate post-exercise recovery.
- **Stress and Immunity:** Immune-boosting IV treatments, particularly those containing vitamin C, zinc, and Glutathione, bolster defenses against seasonal illnesses while promoting relaxation.

Advanced Peptide Therapies

In addition to IV hydration, peptide therapies have gained attention for their potential benefits in elderly care. These treatments are designed to target specific health issues and enhance overall well-being:

- **Buccal Strips BPC-157:** Known for its gut repair and injury recovery properties, this peptide promotes the healing of tissues and reduces inflammation, contributing significantly to recovery processes.
- **CJC-1295:** This peptide aids in muscle tone improvement, anti-aging effects, and better sleep quality, making it a valuable tool in maintaining physical vitality and mental sharpness in the elderly.

- **GHK-Cu:** Focused on skin repair, hair growth, and collagen boost, GHK-Cu contributes to improved skin health and appearance, while also supporting overall cellular health.
- **TA-1:** This peptide plays a critical role in immune system support, making it vital for older adults in preventing infections and maintaining robust immune responses.
- **PT-141:** Known for improving libido and sexual wellness in both men and women, PT-141 adds an important dimension to mental and emotional well-being for the elderly.

We offer and administer these therapies…

A Commitment to Elderly Wellness

In the face of a growing elderly population, the demand for innovative and effective health solutions is increasingly urgent. Dehydration, a preventable issue, can have significant consequences, but it can be mitigated through strategic partnerships and advanced hydration services like those offered by Prime IV Hydration and Wellness. For individuals aged fifty and older, hydration is no longer a matter of simply drinking enough water—it's about ensuring the body functions optimally.

By integrating leading hydration solutions and creating supportive community networks, Prime IV Hydration and Wellness is committed to transforming elderly care. The role of hydration in health and well-being, especially for the elderly, cannot be underestimated. Prime IV continues to lead the charge in providing innovative solutions that renew vitality and enhance life quality. The addition of advanced peptide therapies enhances the approach, offering targeted solutions for specific health concerns and further improving the quality of life for the elderly.

Through these efforts, the journey toward optimal health becomes not just a goal but a reality, demonstrating that the partnership between innovation, community, and personalized care can redefine aging with dignity and vitality.

Angela's Special Offer

Unlock the power of personalized wellness with our IV therapy!

Book a free consultation to explore how customized vitamins, nutrients, minerals, and buccal peptides can boost your health and vitality.

Best IV Therapy in Scottsdale, AZ - Prime IV Hydration & Wellness https://primeivhydration.com/locations/arizona/scottsdale/

Get Any Lab Test Now for Prevention, Care, and Convenience

by Angela Garrett

In the evolving landscape of healthcare, our company, Any Lab Test Now stands out as a pioneer in direct-access lab testing. Since its inception in 1992, our company has been dedicated to providing consumers in the United States with the ability to obtain a wide array of lab tests, without the constraints typically posed by insurance or the necessity of a doctor's order. This innovative model not only democratizes access to healthcare, but also prioritizes immediate and convenient access to essential health information, underpinned by a commitment to affordability and confidentiality.

With over 230 locations nationwide, including the Scottsdale, Arizona site established in 2011, Any Lab Test Now offers a comprehensive suite of lab services. These include TB Skin Testing, fingerprinting for level one fingerprint clearance cards, urinary tract infection tests, PT-INR tests, DNA and relationship testing, hormone panels, and general health screenings. By not accepting insurance, the company maintains a focus on transparent pricing, complemented by the acceptance of

Flexible Spending Accounts (FSA) and Health Savings Accounts (HSA). This approach empowers consumers, allowing them direct control over their healthcare expenses with a clear understanding of costs and without hidden fees.

Understanding the Unique Health Needs of Seniors

As individuals age, the need for consistent health monitoring becomes crucial. Elderly individuals often encounter chronic conditions such as diabetes, heart disease, and osteoporosis. Regular lab testing becomes imperative for early detection of diseases, continuous management of health issues, and providing peace of mind for both seniors and their families.

Convenience and Accessibility

One of the most significant advantages that Any Lab Test Now offers to the elderly is unparalleled accessibility. With widespread locations such as Scottsdale, Arizona, seniors can easily access testing services without needing a doctor's prescription, breaking down substantial logistical barriers. This is particularly beneficial for those with limited mobility.

The availability of walk-in services and the promise of test results within one to three business days facilitate proactive health management. Furthermore, the availability of same-day results for many tests can be crucial for immediate medical decisions. Seniors also benefit from services that include doctor's orders, providing professional insights alongside test results, even in the absence of a personal physician.

Affordability

For seniors living on fixed incomes, affordable lab testing is vital. Any Lab Test Now's pricing model, which does not rely on insurance intermediaries, ensures that essential health tests remain accessible without financial strain. This model proves particularly beneficial for individuals with high insurance deductibles or no insurance coverage at all, as it offers clear and manageable costs.

Comprehensive Health Panels

Targeting the specific health concerns of seniors, Any Lab Test Now offers comprehensive health panels. The Heart Health Panel is designed for early detection and management of heart conditions prevalent in older adults, while the Renal Function Panel monitors kidney health, a common concern as people age. Collectively, these panels provide a thorough overview of critical health markers essential for seniors.

Screening for Common Elderly Conditions

Routine screening tests, such as the Hemoglobin A1c for diabetes management, play a crucial role in managing health conditions common in seniors. The Colorectal Cancer Screening (Blood) Test offers a non-invasive way to detect colorectal cancer, a significant risk for those over fifty, thereby enabling timely interventions and preventive healthcare measures.

Privacy and Professionalism

A commitment to privacy and professionalism underpins the services at Any Lab Test Now, ensuring seniors can access tests confidently. The handling of test results is confidential, affording seniors full control over their medical information. This respect for privacy fosters trust and comfort, reassuring seniors who value autonomy in their healthcare decisions.

Variety of Tests Available

Seniors benefit from the broad variety of tests available at Any Lab Test Now. From general health assessments to tests targeting age-related concerns like vitamin deficiencies, the service offering supports comprehensive health management. The Vitamin D Test, crucial for bone health, helps prevent issues related to aging, thereby supporting optimal health maintenance.

Preventative Health Measures

For the elderly, preventative care is a cornerstone of effective health management. Regular lab testing through Any Lab Test Now assists in identifying early health indicators, enabling seniors to take proactive steps. This preemptive approach not only extends healthy lifespans, but also improves overall life quality by mitigating the impacts of chronic illness.

Comfortable Environment

The welcoming and friendly environment at Any Lab Test Now locations is particularly appreciated by seniors. Designed to be efficient and comforting, these spaces move away from the traditional, intimidating atmosphere of a clinical setting, enabling seniors to focus on their health without undue stress.

Comprehensive Benefits and Empowerment

In summary, Any Lab Test Now provides numerous benefits tailored specifically for the elderly, including accessible locations such as Scottsdale, Arizona, affordability, comprehensive testing options, and a strong emphasis on active health management. By removing traditional barriers to lab testing, the company empowers seniors to manage their health proactively.

The Scottsdale location exemplifies this commitment, continuously serving its community since 2011, and reinforcing Any Lab Test Now's dedication to making healthcare accessible and effective. This strategic alignment of convenience, compassionate care, quick results, and reliable services establishes Any Lab Test Now as an integral player in elderly healthcare. We support independence and optimize health management, while significantly contributing to the quality of life for elderly patients.

Angela's Special Offer

Take control of your health with easy walk-in lab tests! Discover your wellness potential today—no appointment needed, just empowering results. http://anylabtestnow.com/Scottsdale-85258

Hospice and Palliative Care:

Guiding People Through Life's Final Chapter

by Cameron Svedsen

For decades, hospice care has faced steady resistance in the United States. Throughout my work in the medical field, I've always found this puzzling, considering the essential support it offers. Health systems and government agencies devote enormous clinical and financial resources to supporting quality hospice programs, so pushback should be minimal. Yet every hospice agency I've encountered in the greater Phoenix area has met resistance—from patients, families, and providers alike.

My first direct contact with hospice came as a graduate student in social work at Arizona State University in the late '90s. I chose a practicum in the bereavement department of a local hospice, where I met with families who had lost loved ones. I sat with husbands, wives, sons, and daughters as they opened up about the difficulty of living without the person who died. Their grief poured out—remorse, regret, loneliness, and heartache. Yet amid the sorrow, there were also moments of resilience, solace, and resolve.

Patients admitted to hospice during the decline of their health received an essential layer of clinical and emotional support. The bereavement care given to families became a crucial part of their healing process. In counseling sessions, I was often thanked for the bedside work of our hospice team. More than once, I noted in my journal a family's gratitude: "I don't know what I would have done without the hospice team members helping me understand what to expect during my loved one's dying process."

After my hospice internship, I worked in a large hospital that primarily served older adults. I became more comfortable having difficult conversations about death and dying. I encouraged patients to complete advance directives and talk about their wishes with loved ones. That hospital experience eventually helped me transition into the hospice industry, where I became an advocate for earlier enrollment in hospice.

In that new role, I reflected often on my hospital encounters with patients nearing the end of life. What I continually observed was a widespread reluctance to let go of curative treatment and embrace comfort care. Even for patients with extreme, life-limiting conditions, hospital staff went to extraordinary lengths to save lives. As a frontline employee, I absorbed the mindset of treating first and asking questions later—assuming that most people would want to try everything before death.

When I ultimately transitioned into a professional hospice position, my perspective shifted. For the first time, I felt the strong need to advocate for patients and families who wanted a choice. I saw how the system pushed seniors toward surgeries, aggressive treatments, and rehabilitation. While I respected those options for patients who could recover, I lamented the premature rush to provide urgent procedures just to appease a family member or generate higher revenue. In many cases, I became a voice for comfort when advanced treatment only led to more suffering.

Since joining the hospice workforce, I've continued to push for better education around hospice care in Arizona. Many people outside the healthcare industry still don't fully understand the limitations of the human body and why hospice care is a vital form of medical support. The misconceptions are striking. Some believe hospice is simply a physical location where someone goes to die. Others assume hospice assists in hastening death, confusing it with euthanasia. Perhaps most harmful is the myth that hospice is only for the final days of life. Sadly, the national median stay is just eighteen days, even though Medicare's hospice benefit allows up to six months of coverage.

This reality exists largely because community healthcare providers often recommend hospice only in times of crisis. Just recently, I received a call from a nurse practitioner about a long-standing patient whose wife was struggling with advanced dementia. Over the course of four weeks, her decline had been sharp. Her husband reported that she was sleeping more, eating very little, communicating less, and showing increasing confusion. By the time he reached out for help, she was minimally responsive and required total assistance with her daily care. In the final stage of Alzheimer's disease, she was dying.

This case is one of hundreds each year that highlights how our healthcare system fails families at the end of life. This woman should have been referred to hospice much earlier. At any point during the progression of her disease, her neurologist could have suggested hospice or palliative care. If she had been hospitalized, the acute care team could have educated her husband about the services available. Instead, the family was left to wonder whether her decline was simply another phase, rather than the final stage. If they had received disease navigation with a palliative care focus, they could have accessed home-based support much sooner.

Why aren't patients with advanced, incurable illnesses referred to hospice in a timelier manner? Often, it's because medical providers aren't certain when to broach the topic. Whether due to lack of training, fear of difficult conversations, limited time, or financial disincentives, the result is the same: patients and families miss out on care that could ease suffering and provide guidance through one of life's hardest seasons.

After years of speaking about hospice and advocating for earlier use, I came to realize that avoidance goes deeper than physician procrastination or service misunderstanding. It stems from fear—fear of mortality, fear of losing someone, fear of acknowledging decline. Because hospice represents life's conclusion, many people prefer to postpone the discussion entirely.

Part of the resistance also comes from a larger cultural hesitation to talk about death at all. In American society, and particularly in Arizona where many retirees relocate for a fresh start, aging and mortality are often treated as subjects to avoid. We're quick to celebrate longevity but hesitant to acknowledge decline. I've met patients who told me they didn't want their children to see them "give up," as if choosing comfort was somehow a sign of weakness. In reality, facing mortality directly is one of the bravest acts a person can take.

Changing this mindset requires community-level conversations, not just in hospitals and clinics, but in living rooms, places of worship, and senior centers. Scottsdale has a unique opportunity here, with its large retiree population and strong network of healthcare providers. If more families start honest conversations earlier, hospice and palliative care can be viewed not as surrender, but as an affirmation of dignity and choice.

Since these discussions are often delayed, patients with advanced illness continue to be ushered through emergency departments, hospitals, and rehab centers designed to save lives. For those with life-limiting conditions, this cycle only delays the care they truly need and sustains the illusion that a body beyond recovery can somehow be restored.

After watching this cycle repeat for years, I sought to change it. If providers were unwilling to talk about hospice because of stigma, perhaps the answer was to reach patients earlier, while they were still receiving treatment. This is the role of palliative care.

In 2014, I joined a small group of healthcare professionals to build a community-based palliative care company in Arizona. Our goal was to define palliative care as something distinct from hospice, but still meaningful for patients who needed clinical and emotional support. Palliative care allowed us to work with patients still pursuing treatments like chemotherapy or dialysis, while also helping them manage symptoms and anxiety. We created a model where patients and families had more participation in decisions and greater control over their care.

The creation of this service filled an important gap, and we've taken care of thousands of patients over the past twelve years. Still, confusion between hospice and palliative care remains. For providers, recommending palliative care is often a way to acknowledge a patient's need for support without having to say the word "hospice." But the two are different in intent and delivery, and each requires delineation.

Hospice is a fully covered benefit through Medicare and most insurance plans. It includes clinician visits, medications, medical equipment, and supplies related to a patient's terminal diagnosis. Hospice also provides respite for caregivers, dignity for patients unable to care for themselves, and expert support with nutrition, skin care, pain management, and daily needs. Most importantly, it brings nurses, aides, social workers, and chaplains directly into the home to provide emotional, physical, and spiritual support.

Palliative care, on the other hand, is consultative. It's less about hands-on care and more about guidance. A palliative team—often a nurse, social worker, and nurse practitioner—helps patients manage pain, shortness of breath, anxiety, depression, confusion, and other symptoms. The team assists with decision-making, advance directives, and connecting families with community resources such as caregiving or assisted living. While it doesn't replace hospice, it gives patients the support they need earlier, while they are still pursuing treatment.

Both hospice and palliative care are vital pieces of the healthcare system, and both are needed here in Scottsdale. What matters is that patients and families understand their options and feel supported in choosing the type of care that matches their needs and values.

Today, I continue working to improve the training of hospice and palliative care providers locally. Our teams focus on preparing staff to address safety, autonomy, and quality of life for every patient. My hope is that more people in our community will come to see these supportive programs not as a last resort, but as the kind of care everyone deserves when facing serious illness or the end of life. It has been my life's work to guide people through this final chapter, making sure they are met with dignity, compassion, and choice.

Cameron's Special Offer

Families frequently need support in navigating the complexities of today's medical system. To learn more about the home-based care offered through Faith Hospice or Palliative Care Alliance, reach out to Cameron at 602-476-2047 or by email at Cameron.Svendsen@Gmail.com

Managing Transitions With Care

by Cedric Wade

I am the founder of Caring Transitions of Scottsdale, a full-service company specializing in senior relocation, downsizing, estate sales, and home transitions. Serving Scottsdale, Fountain Hills, Carefree, Phoenix, and surrounding areas, my specially-trained team and I are dedicated to making life transitions less stressful and more manageable for families and individuals.

My journey into this business was inspired by personal experience. In 2017, after the passing of a family member, my extended family and I spent months sorting, organizing, and preparing the loved one's home in Wisconsin for an estate sale. Despite the home being tidy, the sheer volume of accumulated items—many still new and unopened—turned the process into a logistical nightmare. That experience planted a seed. When I discovered Caring Transitions, I knew immediately that I wanted to bring its mission to Scottsdale.

Before founding Caring Transitions of Scottsdale, I spent thirty years in the financial services industry, where I helped clients navigate complex decisions with care and integrity. My lifelong commitment to service is also reflected in my community involvement. I am a board member of a global non-profit serving the poor and needy, a former church elder, Sunday school teacher, and short-term missionary.

With a heart for helping and hands-on experience navigating challenging life transitions, I lead Caring Transitions with compassion, professionalism, and a deep understanding of what families go through.

Who We Help

At Caring Transitions of Scottsdale, we are honored to serve a wide range of clients—anyone going through a major life transition who needs compassionate, professional support. While our services are available to everyone, we most often assist clients in the following situations:

- **Senior couples facing health-related transitions:** Often, one spouse is experiencing medical issues that require a move into an assisted living facility. We help manage the entire process—from sorting and packing to resettling—so the transition is as smooth and stress-free as possible.
- **Homeowners downsizing after many years:** Many of our clients have lived in their homes for decades. As time goes on, the upkeep becomes overwhelming, and they decide to move to a smaller home or an independent living community. We assist with organizing, decluttering, and preparing the home for sale.

- **Long-distance family members managing an estate:** When a loved one passes away in the Scottsdale area, and the family lives out of state, for example, in Alexandria, VA, we step in to coordinate everything locally. From clearing out the home and arranging estate sales or auctions to getting the property ready for market, we take care of the details so you don't have to travel back and forth.
- **Surviving spouses needing a fresh start:** In the event of a spouse's passing, the surviving partner may need to transition to a smaller, more manageable home. We provide both the practical support and the compassionate guidance needed during such an emotional time.

No matter the situation, our mission is to ease the burden and bring peace of mind during life's toughest transitions.

Our Process: What to Expect When You Work with Caring Transitions of Scottsdale

We understand that every move or estate clearing is personal—and often overwhelming. That's why we've developed a transparent, step-by-step process to help our clients move forward with clarity, confidence, and peace of mind.

1. **Free In-Home Consultation**

   Every project starts with a personal visit to assess the scope of your situation—whether you're downsizing, relocating, or managing a loved one's estate. After our assessment, we'll leave you with:

   » A clear cost estimate for our services.
   » An estimated return from the estate sale.

» This allows you to make an informed decision about moving forward—no pressure, just clarity.

2. **Organizing, Sorting & Preparing the Home (Days 1–5)**

   Our trained team will sort and organize every area of the home—inside and out—including:

   » Cabinets, drawers, closets, garages, attics, and outdoor spaces.
   » Identifying what will be kept, sold, donated, or discarded.
   » Removing unusable items and donating what can still serve others.

   Each item intended for sale is grouped into a "lot," which could be a single valuable item or a collection of related items bundled for sale.

3. **Professional Photography & Cataloging**

   Once lots are finalized, we:

   » Photograph each lot from multiple angles, including dimensions.
   » Clearly show any blemishes or wear, ensuring full transparency.
   » Assign SKU tags for tracking and easy reference.
   » Conduct research on high-value items like antiques, jewelry, coins, and vehicles.

   - For vehicles, we include a full CARFAX report for buyer confidence.

4. **Online Auction Marketing & Execution**

   We create professional marketing listings and launch your sale on:

   » National estate sale platforms
   » Our own database, reaching up to 50,000+ interested buyers

   Most online auctions run for 5 days (up to 10 for specialty sales). Buyers bid, win, and pay immediately after the auction closes.

5. **Auction Fulfillment & Pickup Day**

   » After the sale: We group and consolidate all items by the winning bidder.
   » A scheduled pickup day is held 2–3 days after the auction closes.

   - Pickup windows are booked in 15-minute intervals to ensure smooth flow.
   - Typically, pickups are scheduled over a 5-hour window.

6. **Final Clean-Out & Broom Clean**

   Once all items are removed:

   » We perform a broom clean of the entire property:

   - Sweep/vacuum floors.
   - Dust surfaces.

   » The home is now cleared and ready for market or turnover to the next owner.

Additional Services We Offer

In addition to estate sales and cleanouts, we offer full transition and relocation support:

- **Professional Packing, Moving and Unpacking**

  We pack your belongings, coordinate the move, and unpack everything in your new home—leaving no boxes sitting around for weeks.

- **POD Packing & Loading**

  Moving out of state? We'll pack and load PODs efficiently and securely.

- **Electronic Space Planning**

  When downsizing, we use digital tools to help you visualize exactly what will fit in your new space—reducing stress and eliminating surprises.

- **Decluttering & Home Organization**

  For clients overwhelmed by the volume of possessions, we offer hands-on help to declutter and organize entire homes, including:

  - Closets
  - Kitchens
  - Garages
  - General living spaces

Why It Works

This process isn't just about logistics—it's about compassion, clarity, and helping people move forward. Whether you're across town or across the country, we make sure every detail is handled with care, transparency, and respect.

Home, on Purpose:

A Family's Worry

by David Endre

It usually starts with a late-night phone call. Mom has fallen again or Dad's cough that seemed harmless yesterday has now landed him in the ER. In the dark hours of the night, headlights cut across the driveway as family members rush to the hospital. Everyone is exhausted, worried, and trying to piece together a plan in the waiting room.

These moments are rarely simple. In the waiting room, siblings debate what to do next. One insists, "Mom can't stay home anymore." Another argues, "She just needs 'a little more help.'" Tension rises, guilt surfaces, and no one feels ready for the decisions ahead. There are whispered prayers, tearful phone calls, and the sinking realization that the family has been caught unprepared.

It doesn't have to be this way. Families can act before an incident occurs, not after it. That's what aging at home, done well, is all about: giving seniors the chance to live safely at home, with purpose in their days and fewer unexpected hospital visits, leading to more tomorrows.That's where an in-home, non-medical senior care agency, like Home Matters Caregiving, steps in.

Why I Do This Work

For more than twenty years, my job in corporate America was to develop continuous improvement cultures. My mantra was always the same: safer, better, faster—in that order. But continuous improvement, for me, was never just about efficiency. It was about people.

At the start of every workshop, I'd ask: "Who had a great day at work today? Yesterday? Last week?" The silence always told me the real story. Then, I'd explain why I was there: to help clear away the daily obstacles so people could go home and tell their spouse, child, or pet, "I had a great day at work today."

My goal was to make individuals' lives better, both at work and at home.When I entered the world of senior care, that philosophy came with me. Only now, we're not just solving workflow problems; we're helping families avoid late-night trips to the ER, easing loneliness, and protecting independence in everyday routines. My mantra has evolved into this: "Safe today. Purpose every day. More tomorrows."

This work is deeply personal. Every family I meet reminds me of my own. I see sons balancing conference calls with doctor visits, daughters stretched between raising kids and caring for parents, spouses who want to help but feel exhausted. Behind every request for care, there is always love, and often, fear. My role, and our agency's role, is to replace fear with confidence.

Supporting Families

Every family wants the same thing: to know Mom or Dad is safe, supported, and able to live at home without lying awake at night worrying.For seniors, it's about safety, routine, and independence. They want to continue doing things that feel familiar. Having their morning coffee in their favorite chair, watching a TV show at the same time every day, or folding laundry because it feels useful. These small acts are the threads of a life well lived.

However, pride often hides the truth. One family told us their parents insisted they were "just fine." Once we stepped in, it became clear they weren't eating balanced meals, had skipped showers, and were falling behind on their medications. It wasn't neglect—it was pride, or fear of being a burden. With gentle support, their parents regained comfort, and the family found peace of mind.

Another daughter said her mom's greatest joy was starting her day with tea on the porch. She didn't want someone hovering. She needed a caregiver to help her dress warmly, steady her steps, and then sit nearby so she felt secure. That small act wasn't about "care" in the clinical sense; it was about preserving her life exactly as she loved it.

A son once shared that what mattered most for his dad wasn't the care itself, but the way it was given. His caregiver didn't just check off tasks; she listened to his stories about the plant, laughed at his long-winded jokes, and helped him feel valued and truly himself.

Families want more than help with tasks. They long for peace of mind, presence, and reassurance that home can remain a place of comfort and meaning.

So how does that vision become reality? Four essentials make the difference:

1. Nurse Guidance Families Can Trust

All home care agencies provide caregivers, but few offer nurse oversight. Families deserve more than an unguided caregiver. They deserve confidence.

With nurse-guided care, families receive:

- **Oversight:** Nurses guide caregivers and tailor care to each senior's needs.
- **Early detection:** Small changes—ankles swelling, a skipped meal, forgotten pills—are caught before they become emergencies.
- **Trusted guidance:** Families can speak directly with someone who knows their loved one personally.

Support for caregivers: Caregivers aren't left alone to guess. They have a professional to back them up.

One family described the difference this way: "Before, we always felt like we were two steps behind. With a nurse checking in, we finally feel two steps ahead."

This approach doesn't just provide care, it provides reassurance. Families know someone is looking ahead, not just reacting in the moment.

2. Purpose Woven into Daily Life

Safety matters, but it's not enough. Seniors deserve purpose—to keep moving, engaging, and enjoying the things that make life worth living.Purpose can be as simple as watering plants, reading the morning paper, or baking their favorite dessert. These activities aren't just pleasant distractions; they protect independence. A body in motion stays in motion, and a spirit engaged stays connected.

One client told us her greatest joy was folding laundry. To her children, it seemed unnecessary. To her, it was proof that she could still contribute. With the right support, she kept that routine, and her sense of usefulness remained intact.

The moments of joy are just as important: puzzles at the table, a grandchild's phone call, a shared laugh. Purpose-driven days prevent the drift into isolation, which can harm just as much as illness.When purpose is part of care, life becomes about what's still possible, not about what's been lost. Families who see their loved ones smiling again realize that purpose is not extra, it is essential.

3. Caregivers Who Keep Growing

At Home Matters Caregiving, learning never stops. Caregivers receive nurse-led classroom instruction and ongoing online training. They sharpen skills in dementia care, safe mobility, and post-illness recovery.

I remember one caregiver who admitted she froze when a client with dementia grew upset. After more training, she guided that same client through a similar moment with calm reassurance. Her growth gave the family confidence too.

Another caregiver described training as the thing that gave her courage. "I don't just feel like I'm on my own," she said. "I know there's a team behind me." That confidence shines through to families, and they feel the difference too. A caregiver who is confident and supported can focus fully on their client, not second-guessing, but caring with assurance.

4. Technology That Extends Peace of Mind

Even the most dedicated families can't be present every moment. Technology quietly fills the gap.Today's monitoring tools are small and always on. They don't require buttons or gadgets to be worn. Instead, they quietly stand watch, identifying changes before they become problems.They can pick up falls, frequent trips to the bathroom, breathing changes, medication mix-ups, and so much more. In some cases, they flag changes so subtle that families or caregivers might otherwise miss them. For one family, it meant that the son could stop calling his dad ten times a day "just to check." He became a son again, not a warden.

Technology doesn't replace in-home care, it extends it. Technology gives families permission to breathe, knowing someone, or something, is always watching over their loved one. For seniors, it's freedom: the ability to live without constant supervision while still being protected.

Real Stories of Support

The best way to understand this approach is through the families who've lived it.

One daughter told us her father had been falling often at night. She felt helpless, waking up again and again to the sound of late-night emergency phone calls. Once monitoring was in place, small changes in her father's movements were flagged. The nurse adjusted care, and the falls stopped. Instead of fear, they found peace of mind.

A son shared how his mother kept landing in the ER with pneumonia. Each hospital stay left her weaker. With nurse oversight and trained caregivers, her cough was caught early. Adjustments were made, and another hospitalization was avoided. For the family, it was a turning point; they no longer lived in fear of the next decline.

These stories show how proactive care turns panic into calm, and fear into reassurance. They are reminders that the little things: a blanket, a steady hand, a kind word, often mean the most.

Recognition That Proves It Works

Families should also know they're not alone in trusting this approach.Locally, Home Matters Caregiving Scottsdale has been recognized as Best of Senior Living 2025 for the fourth year in a row by A Place for Mom. Out of nearly 45,000 providers nationwide, only about one to two percent of home care companies receive this honor, making Scottsdale one of only eighteen agencies nationwide to achieve it.

On a national level, the Home Matters Caregiving family has earned multiple awards—acknowledgments that reflect the same daily reality families describe to us.These awards matter because they confirm what families already feel: that their loved ones are truly in safe hands.

Choosing the Right Partner

So, what should it feel like when you've chosen the right home care agency?It should feel like more than just scheduling hours. The right partner doesn't just send someone to the door, they build care around the person, not just the schedule. It should feel like having a team that understands your loved one's needs and supports them with compassion and skill. The right partner will offer:

- Nurse oversight that brings confidence.
- Purpose woven into daily routines.
- Ongoing caregiver training that adapts as needs change.
- Technology that extends safety and peace of mind.

Choosing the right agency isn't about paperwork or promises. It's about trust: the feeling you get when you know your loved one is truly safe, cared for, and valued.

Families often tell us they thought they were "buying hours of care," but what they really received was something greater: a sense of calm, a return to normalcy, and the freedom to be a son, a daughter, or a spouse again, instead of a constant caregiver.

Aging at home isn't just about today. It's about tomorrow. Families deserve peace of mind, not uncertainty. With the right support, seniors can live safely, add purpose to their days, and share more moments with the people they love.

We believe in planned senior moments—not unplanned ones.*"Safe today. Purpose every day. More tomorrows."*

David's Special Offer

If someone you love wants to keep living safely at home, Home Matters Caregiving is here to help. Call 480-360-3500 or visit https://homematters.com/north-scottsdale-az/ schedule a free consultation today.

Behind the Curtain:

How Your Care is Really Graded

by Doug Sparks

Why This Chapter Matters to You

Most people don't realize it, but every hospital and doctor is being graded on how well they take care of patients. These grades affect how much money they get paid, and more importantly, how much care you and your loved ones actually receive.

The surprising truth? Even when doctors order the right tests, many times the system doesn't follow through. That means patients miss out on services that were already found to be necessary. Families think, "That's just healthcare—always cutting back." But often, it isn't the system cutting care. It's a missed step that can be fixed.

For the same service: A doctor who follows through earns $352, and a doctor who doesn't earns just $179. That's a huge difference, and most providers don't even realize it's happening. Patients end up losing too—because care gets delayed or skipped altogether.

The Good News

Our team has been working for almost two decades on building technology that ensures nothing is missed. We've partnered with leading organizations, like Milliman, to give patients something brand new: access to their own health records, without being trapped behind password-protected portals.It's called My Health Youniverse—a free passport to take control of your health and wellness. For the first time, patients and families can see all their records, compare options, and choose what's best for them.

Why Should You Care?

The best life, health, and travel assurance you and your family can have is keeping your health records in one place—on your own devices. Not scattered across portals. Not hidden behind forgotten passwords. Not lost in hospital systems you can't reach.

In a true emergency, fast access to your records isn't just convenient, it can save your life.

That's why the My Health Youniverse Passport includes My Health Access at no cost. It lets you download, organize, and securely store your personal records—all under your control. And for less than the cost of most TV streaming services, you can subscribe to unlock even more:

- Real-time health record updates from every provider you see, anywhere in the country.
- Unlimited virtual care, right at your fingertips.

For example: if you had ten medical visits in ten different states, every one of those records would update automatically—instantly available to every provider you choose. Your relationships with your doctors don't change. What changes is that *all of them finally see the full picture*—when and how you want them to.Now is the time to take control. Choose your services your way: pay cash, use insurance, subscribe, or mix them however you prefer.Your health. Your choice. Your control.

Why This Is Different

Healthcare leaders—even those running insurance companies—are often shocked when they learn how much is being missed. The truth is, most of them don't know.. But we do, because we helped design the very system they rely on.

That's why we say: Precision is the Ghost in the Machine.

What This Means for You:

- **Better Care:** medically necessary services are actually delivered.
- **No Delays:** health records flow freely, without endless requests.
- **Fairness:** doctors and hospitals get paid correctly, so patients don't lose out.
- **Control:** families finally have access to their own health information.

The Bottom Line

You don't have to accept confusion, delays, or shrinking care. Behind the curtain, there's a system that grades every provider. When it works, it rewards preventive care. When it fails, patients suffer.

The difference now is that you don't have to be left in the dark. With tools like My Health Youniverse, you and your family can finally see the whole picture, take control, and make choices that keep you healthier, longer.Healthcare doesn't have to be complicated. With the right tools, it becomes simple—and it works for you.

The Hidden Grading System in Healthcare

Since 2007, the Co-Founders of Precision Healthcare Technologies have helped design value-based compliance grading platforms in collaboration with CMS (Centers for Medicare & Medicaid Services) and private payers. Today, we track compliance scores on more than 1,061,000 patients, pinpointing—down to the dollar—exactly what services providers have missed.

These aren't optional services. They are mandated services where a medical necessity was proven but not acted upon. Every time that happens, patients miss out on care, and providers lose reimbursement dollars.The good news? We help providers recover those missed opportunities—without upfront costs, without new technology to learn, and without workflow disruptions. Providers gain new revenue, and patients receive the care they deserve.

Precision's Proven Solution

Over eighteen years of technology development and eight years of refining compliance models, we've solved the biggest gap in care coordination: delays caused by locked-down health record requests.Together, with healthcare leader Milliman, we are breaking new ground: for the first time, patients can access their health records outside of password-protected portals. As Dr. Eric Topol predicted in *The Patient Will See You Now*, the future of care is here.

That future has a name: My Health Youniverse. It's your FREE Passport to Control of Your Health & Wellness.

With My Health Youniverse, patients and families can finally see, manage, and use their health information. Options range from free access to subscription care, from insurance coverage, to direct cash-pay choices. Control moves into the hands of the patient.

Here's a true story:

> Three regional presidents from major insurance companies were working to raise Annual Wellness Visit (AWV) completion rates from 40 percent toward 60 percent. But when I explained that even 100 percent completion would still lead to penalties because providers weren't acting on new medical necessities uncovered during those visits, they all stopped and said the same thing: "HUH?!"
>
> They didn't know what they didn't know. And the truth is, most of the healthcare system is in the same boat. Ironically, many of them are relying on systems that we helped

build. That's why we call ourselves: *Precision—The Ghost in the Machine.*

Why This Matters

It's okay to not know what you don't know. But it's not okay to ignore when something directly affects your health, your family, or your finances.Just like the tax code, the system *rewards preventive action* and *penalizes failure* to act when medical necessity is found. Providers don't know where those necessities are buried. But we do, because we built the systems.

A Healthcare Icon's Insight

In one meeting, a healthcare leader who had taken six companies from seed to billion-dollar exits said this:"Gentlemen, I've been in healthcare for fifty years. There aren't thirty people in the country who understand what you've just explained. But you're absolutely right. What can I do to help?"That moment crystallized our mission.

The Five Principles That Guide Us are:

- Exponential exposure to new markets.
- Better service for current patients.
- No upfront or out-of-pocket cost.
- Guaranteed profit.
- Zero disruption to staff workflow.

Our philosophy is simple: *technology is a tool, not the solution.* When "simpler" really is better, we've found the answer.

The Precision Advantage:

- Active in seventeen sectors of healthcare and consumer health.
- Cross-sector connections expand providers' reach and revenue.
- The average provider misses $250,000 annually in compliance-mandated services.
- Precision identifies, documents, and coordinates those opportunities.
- Providers keep all clinical revenue; Precision earns a small fee for coordination.

Where We Start

Our One-Time Compliance & Health Records Engagement Pilot shows immediate results:

- **Expected revenue:** $248,625 in the first 120 days (per 2,500 patients).
- **Average missed revenue:** $583 per patient (based on CMS data).
- Providers recover $100 per patient almost instantly—with no changes to their workflow.

Why the CMS/Payer "Report Card" Matters

Think of the CMS report card like a financial scoreboard. It determines how much money hospitals and providers gain—or lose. On your CMS/Payer "Report Card," you will see things like your RAF score, which acts as your credit score—tied to patient risks and outcomes, and gain access to services proven necessary, but not delivered.

Without Precision, providers are flying blind. With Precision, they can see exactly where they stand—and how to turn penalties into rewards. Healthcare doesn't have to be confusing. It doesn't have to punish patients or providers. By unlocking health records, fixing compliance gaps, and ensuring medically necessary services are delivered, we transform the system. For seniors, caregivers, and families, this means: better care, fewer delays, fairer reimbursements, and a system that finally works for people, not against them.

With urgency and optimism,
The Ghost in the Machine

Adding Life to Years:

Why Movement Matters More than Medicine

by Dr. Molly Powiada

It often starts with something small: a back that stiffens after a walk, a shoulder that aches after a round of golf, a knee that makes the stairs feel harder than they should be. Seniors do the right thing, they go to their primary care doctor. However, the advice is usually the same: "Stop doing the thing that makes it hurt."

So they rest. They stop golfing, or walking, or biking, or lifting their grandkids. The pain fades with rest, and because they love these activities, they try again. The very first time they step back onto the course or trail, the pain shoots right back. Back to the doctor they go, this time leaving with a prescription for injections. The cortisone buys time, six months the first time, three the next, maybe only a few weeks after that. And when the relief runs out, the recommendation becomes surgery.

I have had surgery myself, and let me tell you, surgery is no joke. It takes weeks, often months, to regain even the simplest daily independence. The pain does not always vanish, and sometimes it shifts somewhere else. For too many seniors, that is when the snowball starts. Less activity, more medications, less mobility, less confidence. Slowly, independence and joy slip away.

I have seen this story in my own family. Growing up, my grandpa was the picture of living fully. Some of my best memories are Friday mornings on the golf course with him, followed by Dairy Queen. He walked every morning, golfed multiple times a week, volunteered, and was constantly on the go. Then he hurt his back.

Doctors told him to rest and put him on pain medication. That was over ten years ago. Since then, I have watched him lose the very things that gave his life meaning. He no longer golfs, no longer walks the dogs, no longer lives the vibrant, social life he once had. From the most active, involved grandpa to someone homebound and reliant on medication, it is a transformation that has broken my heart. And it is what drives me to do the work I do every single day. Because it does not have to be this way.

The problem with traditional care is that it almost always chases symptoms. Your shoulder hurts, so all the focus is on your shoulder. Your knee aches, so your knee gets iced, braced, or injected. Rarely does anyone step back and ask, "Why is this happening in the first place?" Without that question, the cycle repeats endlessly: rest, pain, injection, surgery.

At Fortitude Performance Chiropractic, our philosophy is different. We take a whole body approach. We look at how your entire body moves and functions together. We do not just want to quiet pain temporarily, we want to find the root cause, treat it, and give people strategies to prevent it from coming back.

The goal is not simply to reduce symptoms, but to restore confidence, independence, and resiliency.

That is what we did with John. John came to see us after struggling with shoulder pain so severe he could not lift his arm overhead. For him, that meant more than discomfort. John is a golfer. Golf is his passion, his outlet, his social life. It is the time he spends with friends, the way he stays active in retirement, the thing that gives structure and joy to his weeks. But the pain had taken that away. He could not complete a backswing, could not be on the course, could not be with his friends.

John had already tried traditional physical therapy, attending regularly and putting in the effort, but the results were disappointing. After weeks of exercises and treatments, his pain had not improved. When he came to us, it became clear why. All of the attention had been on his shoulder, but the shoulder was not the real problem. John's mid back was stiff and his neck lacked mobility, so his shoulder was left to compensate. Instead of chasing the pain, we worked on the areas that were actually driving it.

The change was remarkable. After only a short time, John's range of motion improved dramatically, and more importantly, his confidence returned. The transformation was not just physical, it was emotional and social. John was able to get back on the golf course. He could swing again, spend time with his friends, laugh, and feel like himself. The isolation that had started to creep in was replaced by connection. The fear that his body was failing him was replaced by belief that it was capable. That is why we do what we do.

Too often, seniors are told that pain is normal, that slowing down is inevitable, that frailty is just part of aging. Especially for women, the narrative becomes even more dangerous. Warnings to "be careful" or "do not lift too much" leave people weaker, more brittle, and more prone to falls and fractures. The truth is the opposite. The strongest protection against frailty is movement. Strength. Mobility. Resiliency.

The same is true with arthritis. People hear the word and assume pain is unavoidable, surgery inevitable. But arthritis is just as normal as gray hair. It is part of aging, but it does not have to mean suffering. What matters more is how well the body moves, how strong the muscles are, and how active the lifestyle is. I have had countless patients come in, told their pain was "just arthritis," and I have watched them walk out weeks later, moving better than they had in decades.

The outcomes we focus on are simple but powerful: staying independent; preventing falls, surgeries, and hospitalizations; building confidence in the body; and giving people the ability to keep doing the things they love. That might mean traveling, golfing, gardening, hiking, playing pickleball, chasing grandkids, or simply being able to get up and down off the floor with ease. Whatever independence and joy looks like for each person, that is the outcome we build toward.

The difference is not just for the seniors, it ripples into their families. When someone is sidelined by pain, it changes everything. Spouses become caregivers. Adult children become chauffeurs. Grandkids see their grandparents sidelined from the very activities that would create lasting memories. I have lived this with my own surgery, depending on my husband for the simplest tasks, and I know how heavy that can feel for both sides. Independence is not just about one person's life, it is about lifting a burden off everyone who loves them.

That is why I see my role in the community as more than just a chiropractor. I am an educator, helping seniors and their families understand that surgery and injections are not the only path. I am a prevention specialist, helping people move better so they do not fall into the cycle of decline. And I am a trusted resource, someone families can come to with questions, knowing they will get honesty, clarity, and support.

What I wish more people understood is the difference between surviving and truly living in those later decades. Surviving means getting through each day dependent on others, homebound, missing out. Living means being present, driving yourself to a game, cheering in the stands, traveling with friends, walking with your spouse, golfing on a Saturday morning, and saying yes when the family invites you on an adventure.

That is what I want for my patients. That is what I want for myself. And that is why I do this work.

Aging is inevitable. Decline is not. You can choose strength. You can choose mobility. You can choose independence. And when you do, you do not just add years to your life, you add life to your years.

I have seen both sides, through my patients, through my grandpa, and through my own surgery. And I know without question which one I want for myself, my family, and every senior I serve.

You deserve more than survival. You deserve to live.

Dr. Powiada's Special Offer

To learn more about how we help seniors stay strong and independent, visit https://go.fortitudephx.com/scottsdale.

There you can explore our resources, download free guides, and schedule a call with Dr. Molly to see how we can support you or your loved ones.

Insurance for Seniors

by John Jefferey and Lynda Carter

With over fifty years combined Medicare, Arizona Medicaid, and health insurance coverage experience, we are the owners of Coordinated Care Consultants LLC. We provide consulting for senior facilities throughout Arizona. We are also the owners of Jeffery Insurance Agency, a full client focused health insurance agency, for senior care coverage options (Medicare), along with individual and family coverages. Together with our Arizona statewide team, we are contracted in twelve states and growing. Recently we were consultants for the launch of the soon to be nationwide Medicaid application software, called Medicaid Soft.

Our doors are open to assist clients with coverage options. We look forward to supporting you! We dedicate this chapter to all Medicare and Medicaid beneficiaries, and our much-loved team of colleagues.

Each state has its own Medicaid program with different names, qualifying rules, and nuances. That said, they all have some common connections on how they work.

Overview:
How Medicare Works—and Where It Stops

Medicare is federal health insurance for most people age sixty-five and older, and for some younger people with disabilities. It has several parts:

- Part A – hospital insurance
- Part B – doctor visits, medical supplies, outpatient care
- Part C – Medicare Advantage plans (private plans that combine A & B, often with extras)
- Part D – prescription drug coverage

Medicare is very helpful, but it *does not pay for long-term care*—the kind of help people need every day with things like dressing, bathing, meals, or supervision.

Here's what it does cover:

- Short-term stays in a Skilled Nursing Facility (SNF) after a qualifying hospital stay (usually at least three days).
- Up to 100 days per benefit period in a SNF if you meet certain rules.
    - » **Days 1–20:** Medicare pays in full (after hospital deductible).
    - » **Days 21–100:** You pay a daily coinsurance.
    - » **After 100 days:** Medicare stops paying.

For long-term care—whether at home, in an assisted living facility, or in a nursing home—seniors often need Medicaid to fill the gap. In Arizona, Medicaid is called AHCCCS (Arizona Health Care Cost Containment System).

AHCCCS for People Sixty-Five and Older

AHCCCS is Arizona's Medicaid program. It has two parts:

1. **Regular AHCCCS**—for general medical coverage.
2. **ALTCS (Arizona Long Term Care System)**—for people who need daily help or nursing home care.

Many seniors have both Medicare and AHCCCS. This is called being "dual eligible." In these cases, Medicare pays first, and AHCCCS may help pay for:

- Medicare premiums, copays, and deductibles
- Some extra services Medicare doesn't cover, like limited dental or medical transport

If you need daily personal care or live in a facility, you may qualify for ALTCS, the long-term care branch of AHCCCS.

ALTCS: Arizona's Long-Term Care Program

ALTCS helps seniors, people with disabilities, and those who are blind who need nursing-level care but can't afford it.

ALTCS may pay for:

- Nursing home care
- Care in assisted living facilities (ALFs)
- Home caregivers or attendants
- Physical, occupational, or speech therapy
- Medical supplies and equipment
- Some home modifications for safety
- Transportation to medical appointments

Medical Eligibility

To qualify, you must need a Nursing Facility Level of Care (NFLOC). This means you need help with several Activities of Daily Living (ADLs) like bathing, dressing, eating, walking, or using the bathroom. Cognitive problems like dementia are also considered, but only if they cause daily care needs.

Financial Eligibility (2025 Rules)

You must also meet income and asset limits.

Applicant Type	Countable Asset Limit	Monthly Income Limit
Single Person	≤ $2,000	≤ $2,901
Married Couple (both applying)	≤ $4,000 combined	≤ $2,901 each
Married (only one applying)	Applicant ≤ $2,000; Spouse keeps a portion called Community Spouse Resource Allowance (CSRA), between $31,584 and $157,920	Same $2,901 income cap applies to applicant

If your income is too high, you may still qualify by using a Miller Trust (also called a Qualified Income Trust) that channels extra income into an approved account.

Arizona also has a five-year "look-back" period. This means ALTCS reviews financial records from the past five years to make sure you haven't given away or transferred assets to qualify. If you have, there can be penalties or a waiting period.

How Medicare and ALTCS Work Together

Many people in Arizona use both programs at different times.

Typical timeline:

1. Hospital stay for at least three days.
2. Short-term rehab at a Skilled Nursing Facility (SNF). Medicare Part A pays up to 100 days.
3. If you still need long-term help afterward, Medicare stops paying, and you may apply for ALTCS.

In summary:

- Medicare = short-term skilled medical care.
- ALTCS (Medicaid) = long-term custodial or nursing care once you qualify.

Even when you are on ALTCS, Medicare continues to cover doctor visits, therapies, and equipment under Parts A and B. ALTCS mainly covers the care and supervision part of living in a facility or at home.

Assisted Living in Arizona

Many Arizona seniors prefer Assisted Living Facilities (ALFs) instead of nursing homes. Here's how coverage works there:

Medicare:

- Does *not* pay for room, board, or daily custodial care in ALFs.
- May still cover some medical services—like therapy, doctor visits, or home health care—if ordered by a doctor.

ALTCS:

- May pay for care services in an ALF if the resident qualifies for nursing-level care.
- Services covered include help with bathing, dressing, meals, medications, and supervision.
- ALTCS usually does not pay for room and board, but it may set limits on what the facility can charge.

Important: Not all assisted living facilities in Arizona accept ALTCS. Always ask whether a facility is ALTCS-contracted before applying or moving in.

Example:
How It Might Work in Real Life

Sarah's Story

Sarah is 82. She breaks her hip and stays four days in the hospital, then moves to a Skilled Nursing Facility for rehab.

1. Short-Term Stay

- Medicare Part A covers the first 20 days in full.
- Days 21–100 require a daily coinsurance payment.

2. Still Needs Care

After rehab, Sarah still needs help with daily tasks. She applies for ALTCS.

3. ALTCS Approval

She meets both medical (nursing-level care) and financial rules (income under $2,901/month, assets under $2,000).

4. Ongoing Care Options

- If she stays in a nursing home, ALTCS covers her care and room/board in a contracted facility.
- If she prefers assisted living and the facility accepts ALTCS, it covers her care services, but she still pays some or all of her room and board.

5. Medicare Still Helps

Medicare continues to pay for doctor visits, therapies, and medical supplies.

6. Out-of-Pocket Costs

Sarah uses her small allowance for personal needs (around $141/month) and pays any remaining uncovered costs until ALTCS begins.

Key Differences in Arizona

Arizona has some unique rules that set it apart from other states:

1. **Income Cap State:**

   The income limit ($2,901/month for singles in 2025) is firm. If your income is higher, you need a Miller Trust to qualify.

2. **Strict Asset & Look-Back Rules:**

   The $2,000 asset cap is low, and ALTCS checks five years of financial history for transfers or gifts.

3. **Spouse Protections (CSRA):**

   If only one spouse applies, the other can keep some assets (between about $31,000 and $157,000).

4. **Facility Contracts:**

   Only certain nursing homes and ALFs accept ALTCS. Always check contracts before applying.

5. **Room & Board Costs:**

   ALTCS may limit what facilities can charge, but residents often still pay most room and board costs themselves.

6. **Managed Care System:**

   ALTCS is managed through private insurance contractors. Members enroll in a plan that coordinates their care, providers, and facilities.

7. **Home & Community-Based Services (HCBS):**

   ALTCS also supports care at home or in small group homes, helping people stay out of institutions when possible.

Financial Planning & Cost Expectations

Many seniors must plan carefully before qualifying for ALTCS or to pay what it doesn't cover. Here are a few key points:

- **Medicare SNF coinsurance:** After 20 days, you pay about $209.50 per day (2025 rate) for days 21–100.
- **Assisted living room & board:** Can range from $3,000 to $6,000+ per month, depending on location and services. ALTCS may cover care services but not housing.
- **Personal Needs Allowance:** ALTCS members can keep a small monthly allowance (around $141) for personal spending.

- **Income trusts:** If your income is too high, a Miller Trust can help you qualify.
- **Married couples:** The Community Spouse Resource Allowance helps protect assets for the spouse who stays at home.
- **Private pay before ALTCS:** You may need to use savings or pensions for care until you meet eligibility.

Policy and Current Challenges in Arizona

Arizona faces some ongoing issues around senior care and long-term care programs:

- **Tight Financial Limits:** Many middle-income seniors earn too much for ALTCS but can't afford private long-term care.
- **Limited ALTCS Facilities:** Some areas, especially rural ones, have few contracted facilities.
- **Quality Concerns:** Oversight and staffing in assisted living and nursing homes are ongoing priorities.
- **Estate Recovery:** After death, the state may recover costs from the person's estate for Medicaid-funded care. Families should plan for this.
- **Awareness Gaps:** Many families don't realize Medicare doesn't cover long-term care until a crisis happens.
- **Policy Proposals:** Arizona continues to explore ways to improve ALTCS reimbursement rates, expand home care options, and simplify eligibility.

Practical Tips for Arizona Seniors & Families

1. **Plan Early**

   Don't wait for a hospital stay or sudden illness. Review your health, finances, and possible long-term care needs in advance.

2. **Understand Medicare Limits**

   Medicare covers short-term rehab, not long-term custodial care. Know how many SNF days you've used in each benefit period.

3. **Check Facility Participation**

   Before choosing an assisted living or nursing home, confirm it accepts both Medicare (for skilled care) and ALTCS (for long-term care).

4. **Apply for ALTCS When Needed**

   Start the process early—it takes time for medical and financial reviews. Contact your local AHCCCS office or an ALTCS representative.

5. **Use a Miller Trust if Needed**

   If your income is slightly above the limit, talk to an elder-law attorney about setting up a Miller Trust.

6. **Budget for What's Not Covered**

   Plan to pay for room and board, personal expenses, and any small medical costs not covered by Medicare or ALTCS.

7. **Legal & Estate Planning**

   Get help setting up power of attorney, advance directives, and estate documents. Know how Medicaid estate recovery works in Arizona.

8. **Explore Home Care Options**

   ALTCS offers in-home care for eligible seniors who want to stay in their own homes.

9. **Use Case Managers & Local Resources**

   ALTCS provides case managers to help coordinate services. Nonprofits like AARP Arizona and local elder-law clinics can also help families navigate the system.

With preparation, the right information, and support from professionals or case managers, Arizona seniors and their families can find quality, affordable care that fits their needs.

Jeffery Insurance and Coordinated Care Consultants team of professionals can help with Arizona state Long Term Care application assistance, Long Term Care contracted carrier assignment, Medicare Special Needs plan selection and enrollment assistance, mobile, home visiting medical providers and more . . .

John Jeffery's Special Offer

At Jeffery Insurance Agency, we believe choosing health insurance should feel like a step toward peace of mind—not a burden. With personalized guidance and plans that fit your life, we're here to help you feel confident about your coverage."50 years of excellence".

Call: 480-489-2937 or visit:

http:// www.JefferyInsurance.com

Compassion Meets Technology:

Supporting Older Adults at Home

by Kendra Seavey

Across the globe, the number of older adults is growing faster than ever before. As people live longer, they share a common wish: to remain in their own homes, connected to their communities, and as independent as possible. Yet aging in place brings its own challenges: risks of falls, isolation, medication mismanagement, and the emotional and physical strain on family caregivers. Technology holds tremendous promise in addressing these challenges—not by replacing human care, but by augmenting it and creating a compassionate network of support.

As the CEO of care.coach, I've had the privilege of working at the intersection of aging services, healthcare, and technology for many years. What I've learned is that the most impactful solutions aren't simply "high-tech." They are high-touch through technology. The best tools are empathetic, responsive, and deeply human, even when powered by digital innovation.

When my grandmother, *Mimi*, was in her later years, she remained fiercely independent. She had lived in her home for decades, hosting family dinners, tending her garden, and sewing gifts for everyone she loved. But as she aged and my grandfather passed, I began to see small cracks forming: increased anxiety, missed medications, not drinking enough water, and fewer opportunities for social connection.

When I would call her, she often sounded sad and anxious about what was ahead. I wanted to offer her a companion, not a nurse or a machine, but a gentle voice and friendly presence. Someone, *or something*, who could watch over her in the quiet hours and simply *be there* when no one else could.

That experience deepened my passion for the work we do at care. coach. It made me want to help bring this kind of connection and support to more families across the U.S.—to people like my Mimi, who deserve to age with comfort, companionship, and dignity.

This chapter explores how technology can help older adults stay safer and healthier at home, ease the burdens of caregiving families, and empower organizations like care.coach to reshape the future of aging—through real, human-centered impact.

Technology as a Safety Net

I've worked with many families over the years, and I often hear them describe caring for an aging parent as being "on alert" 24/7. They worry about safety risks like falls, loneliness, or medical emergencies. For families living at a distance, that worry is compounded by the lack of daily visibility into their loved one's well-being.Technology can fill that gap by creating a layer of support that never sleeps.

Today, innovations such as remote monitoring, AI-driven coaching, medication reminders, wearable devices, and telehealth platforms allow older adults to maintain independence while families gain peace of mind. Yet for all these advancements, one key challenge remains: engagement. Devices only work if they are used consistently. Older adults are more likely to embrace technologies that feel approachable, supportive, and non-judgmental.

At care.coach, we've built our platform around this principle. Rather than focusing solely on sensors or alarms, we focus on relationships. Our digital avatars—friendly, animated pets—serve as the bridge between advanced technology and the everyday lives of older adults. Through these avatars, our platform delivers coaching, reminders, health monitoring, and companionship in a way that feels personal and natural.

The care.coach Approach

The foundation of care.coach is deceptively simple: an engaging avatar on a tablet that "lives" with the older adult. But behind that avatar is a powerful combination of human care team members and intelligent technology.

- **24/7 Support:** the avatar is always available to provide reminders, encouragement, and companionship.
- **Health and Safety Monitoring:** our care team receives real-time information, allowing us to intervene early when issues arise.
- **Family Connection:** families receive updates and can rest assured that their loved one is never alone.

- **Engagement First:** by blending warmth, humor, and empathy into every interaction, the avatar feels less like a device and more like a supportive companion.

This approach addresses not only clinical needs, but also the most human ones: to be seen, heard, and valued.At care.coach, we often talk about human-centered technology. For me, that concept is deeply personal. Every avatar, reminder, and intervention keeps my Mimi in mind.The avatar isn't just a coaching tool, it represents what I wish had been there for Mimi in her quietest moments. Its friendly voice might have reminded her to take her medication or simply offered a kind word when she felt alone.

Outcomes That Matter

Technology must ultimately prove its value through outcomes. In our work with PACE, Program of All-Inclusive Care for the Elderly, organizations, long-term care providers, and families, care.coach has demonstrated measurable results:

- **Improved Medication Adherence:** participants receiving avatar reminders are significantly more likely to take their medications on time.
- **Reduced ER Visits and Hospitalizations:** early detection of issues—such as unusual sleep patterns, skipped meals, or changes in mood—has led to timely interventions, preventing costly and traumatic hospitalizations.
- **Enhanced Mental Well-Being:** many older adults report feeling less lonely and more connected thanks to the companionship of their avatars.

- **Family Caregiver Relief:** families consistently share that care.coach provides peace of mind and reduces caregiver stress.

One daughter told us: "For the first time in years, I can sleep through the night without worrying if my mom is okay. I know she has someone looking out for her."

Stories of Impact

Our stories bring data to life. Claire, a participant in her 80s, was struggling with isolation after her husband passed away. She was hesitant about technology but quickly warmed to her care.coach avatar, a cheerful digital dog. Over time, the avatar encouraged her to take her medications, participate in daily exercises, and re-engage with her knitting hobby. Her daughter said, "Mom laughs again. That's something we hadn't seen in years."

Our service helped another participant, Charlie, get the care he needed in a dire situation. One evening, the care.coach system detected unusual behavior in Charlie—confusion and repeated mentions of dizziness. Our care team escalated the concern, and Charlie's family was able to get their father to the hospital quickly, where doctors treated a minor stroke. The attending physician told the family, *"If you hadn't caught this when you did, the outcome could have been far worse."*

*Mary, a*nother participant, used her avatar as a way to rebuild confidence after a fall. The avatar provided encouragement during physical therapy exercises and reminded her to use her walker. Over several months, her strength improved, and she regained her independence.

These stories illustrate the human side of technology, how a simple interaction can become a lifeline, a motivator, and a source of comfort.

Beyond Wages and Workforce: Supporting Human Caregivers

One of the most pressing challenges in aging services is the workforce shortage. Even the most dedicated staff cannot be everywhere at once, and caregiver burnout is a constant concern. Technology provides not just a safety net for older adults, but also a support system for the human caregivers behind the scenes.

By handling routine reminders, check-ins, and companionship, care.coach allows professional staff to focus on higher-level care needs. Families, too, are freed from the anxiety of constant vigilance. Instead of spending every moment worrying, they can spend more time simply *being present* with their loved one.

Looking Ahead: The Future of Technology and Aging

The future of technology in aging is not about replacing people with machines, it's about creating hybrid systems of care. As artificial intelligence, virtual reality, and digital health tools evolve, we must continue to anchor them in empathy, dignity, and humanity.

At care.coach, our vision is to expand these capabilities: integrating predictive analytics, deepening family engagement, and ensuring that even the most vulnerable older adults can access support regardless of socioeconomic status.We believe technology, when used thoughtfully, can help older adults live not just longer, but *better.*

In the future I imagine, every older adult will have access to a gentle companion rooted in care and dignity. I envision a world where the quiet loneliness my Mimi faced is rare. Where families don't sleep in fear, but in trust.

I carry Mimi with me in every initiative we take, every avatar we design, and every partnership we build. Because behind every piece of technology is a human life, and for me, behind care.coach is the voice of a granddaughter who wanted to protect, comfort, and keep her beloved grandmother safe, seen, and cared for.

Technology with Heart

Supporting older adults at home is about more than monitoring, it's about caring. Technology offers incredible opportunities to make homes safer, healthier, and more connected, but its greatest power lies in its ability to deliver comfort, recognition, and reassurance.

As we've seen at care.coach, when technology is designed with empathy, it doesn't feel like technology at all. It feels like a companion, a safeguard, and a bridge between generations. For families, it means peace of mind. For older adults, it means dignity, independence, and the joy of living a full life in their own homes.

Kendra's Special Offer

As we rethink aging in place, I encourage you to explore how thoughtful technology can support your loved ones' independence and safety. Small steps—like connecting with human-centered solutions—can make a meaningful difference in their quality of life and peace of mind for your family. Visit: Care.coach™ | Virtual Companionship & Health Coaching for Seniors

How We Protect Seniors from Fraud and Scams Every Day

by Malea Madrid

Fraud and scams are growing at an alarming rate. Seniors are among the most heavily targeted, losing an estimated $36B every year to con artists and predators.For me, this issue is personal. I'm Malea, founder of Consider It Done Seniors (CID Seniors) and the Golden Rule Alliance. My journey started simply: helping my grandparents with their bills, paperwork, and mail. I saw how easily seniors could be overwhelmed by financial details and how quickly scammers could slip through the cracks.

What started as a granddaughter helping her family, grew into CID Seniors, a company dedicated to protecting older adults. Later, I launched the Golden Rule Alliance, a nonprofit fighting for stronger protections nationwide.Every day, my team and I step into the lives of seniors—not just to educate them, but to stand beside them, sort their mail, reconcile their accounts, catch fraud early, and give them peace of mind.

The Challenge Seniors Face

Scammers know seniors are often isolated, grieving, or overwhelmed by paperwork and technology. That's why they are targeted with:

- Phone scams demanding urgent payments.
- Mail fraud disguised as official documents or charity requests.
- Tech support scams that take over computers and drain accounts.
- Predatory real estate schemes that pressure seniors into selling homes for less than they're worth.

The problem isn't just education. Seniors can know the risks and *still* fall victim because scammers exploit trust, fear, or confusion. That's why they need more than tips. They need a trusted partner in their daily lives.

How We Help: Daily Money Management in Action

At CID Seniors, we provide Daily Money Management (DMM). This is the hands-on work of protecting seniors' finances and dignity day by day. Here's what that looks like in practice:

- **Sorting Mail and Spotting Danger:** Many scams arrive by mail. We sit down with clients, open envelopes, and separate real bills from junk or fraud.One client received a letter from a bank asking for more information to process a loan she never applied for. Because we caught it in time, we froze her credit, alerted the bank, and stopped the fraudulent loan before it went through.

- **Reviewing Accounts and Catching Errors:** Seniors often miss fraudulent charges because statements are confusing. We reconcile every account, every month. We once noticed strange activity in a client's checking account—charges she didn't recognize. Because we caught them early, the bank was able to reverse the charges and close the compromised account.
- **Protecting Homes and Assets:** Scammers target the most valuable asset many seniors own: their home.
- One of our clients was conned into selling her house for $120,000 less than it was worth. We stepped in, uncovered what happened, and were able to get her home back for her. Without intervention, she would have lost everything.
- **Managing Bills and Reducing Clutter:** We organize bills, ensure they're paid on time, and close unnecessary accounts. This reduces stress and leaves fewer openings for scammers.
- **Helping with Insurance and Medical Claims:** Medical bills are a common source of confusion and exploitation. We review insurance statements, challenge errors, and make sure seniors only pay what they truly owe.
- **Creating Budgets and Oversight Systems:** By tracking income and expenses, we help seniors feel in control and give families reassurance that everything is accounted for.

This isn't just paperwork. It's prevention. Many scams succeed only because no one is watching closely. Our services put a trusted second set of eyes on every detail.

Stories of Protection

To understand how this works, here are some stories from my own work:

Mr. Golden, an eighty-three-year-old man, widowed and lonely, trusted his massage therapist. Over time, she gained power of attorney and placed herself on the deed to his home. Despite reaching out to multiple authorities, no one would act because he was considered "vulnerable." He felt trapped and hopeless, and he ended his life.That story haunts me. It showed me how broken the system is—and why seniors need proactive, everyday protection before things reach that point.

In another situation, after losing her only son, Nicole moved in with her daughter-in-law. Instead of helping, the daughter-in-law drained Nicole's accounts and sold her possessions. Nicole was left with almost nothing, and legal help was out of reach.This is why CID Seniors exists—so someone is checking, asking questions, and protecting seniors before an abusive contact of theirs takes everything.

We encountered another case where a respected church member, overwhelmed by caregiving responsibilities, was convinced by a neighbor to sell his home for nearly $400,000 under value. Because he was not considered vulnerable, no protection was offered.Contrast that with our client whose home sale we stopped in the previous section. The difference? We were there to catch it.

Competent Yet Vulnerable

The biggest gap in the system is this: the law only protects seniors if they have a mental defect, in my experience that means they are declared incompetent. But vulnerability doesn't always mean incompetence. A senior may:

- Be grieving a spouse.
- Struggle with stress or depression.
- Feel overwhelmed by paperwork.
- Lack knowledge of technology.
- Trust the wrong person at the wrong time.

These seniors are fully competent, but they are also at risk, which the law doesn't recognize. That's why I launched the Golden Rule Alliance: to expand the definition of "vulnerable adult" in state and federal laws. Our Golden Rule Alliance advocates for three changes:

- **Expand the Definition of Vulnerability:**
    - » Protect competent seniors who are situationally vulnerable—due to grief, stress, tech challenges, or isolation.
- **Truth and Disclosures Act:**
    - » Require plain-language contracts and disclosures. Seniors deserve to understand what they're signing.
- **Accountability and Oversight:**
    - » Give Adult Protective Services more authority.
    - » Hold corporations and individuals accountable when they enable exploitation.

This advocacy is fueled by the stories I've lived. I know what happens when no one steps in. That's why I'm pushing for systemic change. It's not just seniors who benefit from daily money management—it's families too.

Why Families Rely on Us

Knowing the seniors in their lives are protected by our services, families experience:

- **Peace of mind:** Adult children know their parents' bills are paid, their accounts are monitored, and someone is watching for fraud.
- **Less stress:** Seniors feel supported, not judged. They keep their independence while knowing help is available.
- **Better communication:** We often serve as a bridge between seniors, their families, and professional advisors.

One daughter told me, "I sleep better knowing you're going through Mom's mail. I don't have to worry about her falling for the next scam that shows up."

Practical Tips for Seniors and Families

While professional help is the strongest safeguard, here are steps anyone can take:

- **Screen calls:** Let unknown numbers go to voicemail.
- **Pause before acting:** Scammers push urgency. Take time to confirm.
- **Check with someone you trust:** A quick second opinion can prevent disaster.
- **Use secure bill pay:** Paying directly through the bank is safer than automatic deductions from companies.
- **Shred junk mail:** It removes temptation and reduces risk.
- **Report scams:** Even if you can't get the money back, reporting builds data to protect others.

Protecting Seniors, Preserving Dignity

Fraud and scams aren't just about stolen money. They rob seniors of dignity, trust, and independence.Through CID Seniors, I've made it my mission to protect seniors where they're most vulnerable: in their daily lives. By reviewing mail, reconciling accounts, stopping fraudulent loans, and even reversing unfair home sales, we provide real defense.

Through the Golden Rule Movement, I'm pushing for broader change—laws that protect not just the incompetent, but the competent yet vulnerable. It all comes back to the Golden Rule: treat others as you'd want to be treated. One day, each of us will grow old. Will we have protections in place, or will we face the same risks our seniors face today?

The choice is ours. And the time to act is now.

Malea's Special Offer

Stand with us to protect seniors! Get organized with Consider It Done Seniors to stop fraud before it starts, and join the Golden Rule Alliance to demand stronger laws that safeguard vulnerable adults.

Visit https://cidseniors.com/ call 602-671-3623, or email Admin@CIDSeniors.com to take action today.

Medicare Decisions:

A Client's Journey

by Marcus Moran

As an insurance broker, I often hear clients say, "What do I do?" or "This Medicare stuff is so confusing." The confusion isn't surprising. The information provided is often vague, or written like a rulebook filled with scenarios that may or may not apply to them.

To bring this to life, let me introduce a client named Deb. Her Medicare journey mirrors the questions and concerns many others face when making this important decision.

Deb's concerns centered around what she called "good care." For her, that meant continuing to use the providers she already trusted and being able to see any doctor she wanted, without restrictions. Her second concern was cost: being able to afford health insurance as retirement approached. Lastly, Deb admitted her health was not perfect and likely wouldn't improve as she aged. She needed a plan that gave her freedom while also being financially predictable."Does that even exist?" she asked.

If you can relate to Deb, let's look at some solutions and practical steps—ones that turned a broker–beneficiary relationship into a lifelong friendship.

Why Deb's Decision Matters

Deb's Medicare decision—like yours—is critical. It determines how healthcare will be delivered for the rest of your life. Medicare was designed as a *lifetime* healthcare plan, not a year-to-year decision.

Yet today's Medicare landscape often forces seniors to make annual plan changes, sometimes with irreversible consequences. This is especially concerning for those facing cognitive decline or health challenges.

The fact that we ask seniors to make these complex choices every year only highlights how crucial the *initial* decision is. So how can you, like Deb, navigate this minefield while protecting yourself in a rapidly changing environment?

Knowledge or Partnership

Your first step is either to acquire knowledge or to form a partnership with a Medicare insurance broker.Deb chose the latter after a mutual friend recommended me. With some basic knowledge in hand, she set a meeting to talk through her options.Together, we started with a simple checklist of what mattered most to her:

- **Choice:** Do you want to choose your providers, or are you comfortable with your insurance company making those decisions?
- **Control:** Do you want control over who you see, when you see them, and how often?
- **Cost:** Will your premiums protect you from dipping into long-term savings if healthcare costs rise?

Medicare Advantage vs. Original Medicare

While Medicare offers a variety of plans, the most common decision comes down to: Original Medicare, with or without a Supplement/Medigap Plan, or Medicare Advantage. If you have military service or a state/federal retirement plan, your choices may differ, but for most people, these are the two main options.

Medicare Advantage can be appealing if you can count on two things: your health and cognitive state remain stable and your provider networks remain stable. The biggest draw is the cost. Many Medicare Advantage plans have zero or very low premiums. That's attractive to retirees facing reduced income. These plans also offer perks not included in Original Medicare, such as gym memberships, Part B premium reductions, dental, and vision coverage.

For savvy consumers, comparing networks, co-pays, and maximum out-of-pocket costs can reveal good value. But here's the catch: can sixty-five-year-old Deb be certain that seventy-eight-year-old Deb will *still* want—or be able—to navigate this marketplace every year?

Deb liked the idea of zero premiums and wanted to know: "Can I freely move between Original Medicare and Medicare Advantage?"Here's the reality: When you first enroll in Medicare, you can choose Original Medicare or Medicare Advantage without medical questions. After your first year, moving back to Original Medicare may require medical underwriting if you want a Supplement (Medigap) plan.

For example, if Deb starts with Medicare Advantage and later wants to switch to Original Medicare, she would likely want a Supplement plan to cover the 20 percent Medicare doesn't pay. At that point, she could be denied coverage based on her health. If denied, her best option would be to remain in the Advantage plan. In other words, her future health could limit her choices.

A Strategic Approach

So, how can someone like Deb protect herself?My advice: start with Original Medicare and add a Supplement plan. This combination covers hospitalization, skilled care, and ongoing therapy—while giving you maximum choice and control.If your health declines, your coverage remains comprehensive. And just as important, this decision brings *peace of mind* during an uncertain transition.

Later, if finances become tight, you can always move into a Medicare Advantage plan, since those plans don't require health questions to join.This approach gives you the best of both worlds: strong protection upfront, with flexibility to adjust later.

What Is the Broker's Responsibility?

A broker's role can be summarized into three main responsibilities:

- **Onboarding and Ongoing Support:** This includes answering questions, guiding clients through procedures, and reassuring them that they made the right decision. These conversations can range from "Is this covered?" to, "Can you explain what my Explanation of Benefits statement means?"
- **Market Research and Updates:** Brokers monitor the marketplace to identify better opportunities or changes that

could benefit clients. This ensures clients remain informed and positioned to take advantage of favorable options.
- **Annual Reviews:** Typically conducted during the Medicare Annual Enrollment Period in the fall. Too often, I hear clients say they have not heard from their agent or assume everything is fine simply because no one reached out. Annual reviews help prevent missed opportunities and ensure continued alignment with client needs.

The rules and details of Medicare Part D often confuse and frustrate clients. Many people have heard stories about missed deadlines, penalties, or even loss of coverage. My role is to simplify this process and help clients make confident decisions.

Here are a few basics to keep in mind:

- **Annual Enrollment:** Part D plans can be changed each year from October 15th through December 7th.
- **Other Opportunities:** While other windows and special election periods exist, these dates apply to most beneficiaries.
- **Importance of Review:** Reviewing coverage during this time is highly recommended. If medications haven't changed, the plan may not need to be updated. However, reviews often reveal opportunities to save money through a new plan or by switching pharmacies.

Because plan formulas change every year, it's important to remain flexible and open to adjustments. Unfortunately, I sometimes meet referrals who were never guided through this review process. These conversations can be difficult—especially if deadlines have been missed or penalties applied—but at that point my responsibility is to explain the situation clearly and present any possible alternatives.This is why speaking with a broker is so critical: you gain access to accurate, timely information to maximize your coverage and avoid costly mistakes.

Why I Do What I Do

Helping seniors navigate Medicare is more than a profession, it's a calling. I approach every client as if they were my own parent, and I am committed to giving advice that aligns with their unique goals and expectations for health coverage.

I've found that building strong, lasting relationships is far more rewarding than chasing commissions. When clients trust you and feel cared for, they often refer you to their family and friends. This creates a cycle of meaningful partnerships built on trust and mutual respect.

If you are reading this, you are likely curious, have questions, or want to build a relationship with a broker who values honesty and your best interests. I look forward to being that trusted partner.

Marcus's Special Offer

I am offering a comprehensive Medicare Planning conversation free of charge to those that reach out and would like to take advantage of this offer. This process is about 45 minutes to 1 hour, in person, via zoom or the phone.

How Advanced Home Watch Services, LLC Supports Seniors and Their Families

by Patty Knox-Hermann

When I founded Advanced Home Watch Services, my original purpose was simple: to give seasonal homeowners—our valley's snowbirds—peace of mind while they were away. I wanted them to know their homes were safe, secure, and ready for their return. What I didn't realize at the time was that this service would open the door to an even greater calling.

As I responded to more concierge requests: stocking refrigerators before arrivals, coordinating service providers, preparing homes before storms, I began to see a growing need much closer to home. Seniors who had chosen to age in place were facing unique challenges. Many wanted to remain independent, but simple tasks like checking for leaks, managing repairs, or preparing their homes after hospital stays were becoming overwhelming.

It was in these moments that I realized Advanced Home Watch Services could serve a much deeper purpose. Beyond caring for vacant homes, we could stand in the gap for seniors and their families, providing the watchful care that allows aging loved ones to remain safe, comfortable, and confident in their own homes.

The Hidden Risks of Aging in Place

The desire to age in place is tied to dignity and independence. But while familiar surroundings provide comfort, they can also hide risks.Small issues—like a slow leak under a sink, a faulty AC unit, or pests entering through worn seals—may seem minor but can quickly become emergencies. In Arizona's heat, an air conditioning failure is not just an inconvenience; it's dangerous. A burst water heater or mold from a hidden drip can create a major health crisis, and may force seniors from their homes.

Beyond the physical risks, uncollected mail or packages left outside can draw the wrong kind of attention. These details, easy to overlook, can leave seniors vulnerable. Family members often assume a quick neighborly check will suffice, but trained eyes and systematic inspections are what prevent crises.

What Is Professional Home Watch?

Professional home watch service goes far beyond a neighbor peeking through a window. It is a structured, accredited service built on accountability and integrity that looks at the client's home with a set of trained eyes to catch the obvious and not-so-obvious issues a senior homeowner may have missed.

Each home check follows a detailed checklist: scanning for water damage, HVAC performance, pests, possible electrical concerns, and security issues. Reports are documented with photos so families know exactly what is happening. Unlike informal arrangements, a professional home watch service is insured, bonded, and nationally accredited.

This accreditation matters. It reassures families that the service is consistent, thorough, and backed by professional standards. The difference between casual oversight and Advanced Home Watch Services is often the difference between catching a small problem early, or facing costly, disruptive repairs later.Our motto, "Watchful care while you're there," is more than a phrase. It reflects the role we play in preserving independence, safety, and peace of mind while aging in place.

What's Offered by Advanced Home Watch Services

At Advanced Home Watch Services, we tailor our support to each family, blending property care with personal touches.

- **Routine Home Checks:** Weekly or biweekly walkthroughs catch issues early. For example, while checking a client's home, I noticed a small amount of water leaking into the pan under the water heater. Because it was caught in time, repairs were quick and my client was spared displacement. I walk the entire property inside and out, checking for a whole host of things. From hose bib leaks, pests, pest damage, to failing windows, just to name a few.
- **Concierge Services:** Comfort matters as much as safety. From stocking refrigerators to preparing homes after hospital stays, concierge care reduces stress. One client returned from rehab to find fresh groceries, clean linens, and a comfortable setting—a soft landing instead of a stressful one.

- **Seasonal and Emergency Support:** Monsoon storms and extreme heat pose real risks. We prepare homes ahead of time and respond quickly after emergencies. After one storm, we coordinated roof repairs before the next rain could seep in, protecting both property and health.
- **Vendor Coordination:** Many seniors struggle to find reliable service providers. We act as advocates, ensuring quality and fairness. When a pest issue wasn't resolved by one company, we stepped in with trusted partners and oversaw the work until the problem was solved.
- **Customized Care Plans:** Every family is different. Some seniors need weekly checks, others need seasonal prep, and we have those who require full oversight. Plans are flexible, designed to meet needs without overwhelming families.

Together, these services do more than protect property—they safeguard the independence and well-being of seniors who want to remain in the homes they love.

How Advanced Home Watch Services Supports Seniors & Their Families

The practical benefits of a professional home watch service are clear, but the emotional benefits are just as powerful.

- **Peace of Mind for Families:** Adult children often live far from their parents and carry constant worry. One daughter told me she finally slept through the night after knowing her mother's home was being checked regularly. Families can focus on relationships instead of fear.

- **Preserving Dignity:** Many seniors resist help, fearing it means losing independence. By centering our work on the home, we quietly protect the person. Seniors retain autonomy, while families know safety isn't being compromised.
- **A Trusted Circle of Care:** Our role often extends beyond inspection. We learn routines, know what matters, and become a trusted presence. For one senior, visits became a source of connection as well as care, reassuring both her and her children that she was not alone.

The ripple effect is profound: seniors feel secure, families feel less burdened, and generations can enjoy more time together without the shadow of constant worry.

Case Studies & Real-World Scenarios

Stories show the heart of what we do.A senior living alone was unaware of a drip under the kitchen sink. Left unchecked, it would have created mold and a health hazard. We caught it early, and repairs were quick, preventing a crisis and saving the family stress and expense.

Another client of ours, an active senior couple, use walkers to get around, so walking around their yard isn't always easy. During our weekly check, we found a broken sprinkler head flooding the sideyard. We were able to stop the water and call the landscaper for repair.

Sometimes it's not about preventing disaster, but creating comfort. A widow returning from surgery found her home prepared: groceries stocked, linens fresh, thermostat set just right. Her children described it as "the gift of a soft landing."

Looking Ahead: Planning for the Future

Too often, families wait until a crisis forces decisions: an accident, a hospitalization, or sudden home damage. Planning ahead avoids panic and preserves control.Being proactive is not about fearing the future; it's about embracing it with confidence. Systems like having a professional home watch service create a safety net that allows seniors to remain independent, while families know the home environment is safe and supportive.

A cared-for home is more than shelter: it is where memories are made, where laughter echoes, and where legacies are built. By preparing now, families give themselves the freedom to focus on connection, joy, and togetherness.

Aging in place is a profound choice, one that deserves the right support. Without safeguards, small issues can escalate into crises that disrupt independence, health, and finances.That is why Advanced Home Watch Services exists. Through home checks, concierge care, vendor coordination, and customized plans, we provide more than a checklist—we provide peace of mind. Seniors remain safe at home, and families are reassured that someone is watching over the details.

Our mission—watchful care while you're there—reflects both the protection of property and the preservation of dignity. And we do not do it alone. We partner with a trusted network of professionals: handymen, plumbers, electricians, roofers, pest control experts, and house cleaners, so when issues arise, families don't scramble. The right help is already in place.

By bridging the gap between independence and safety, we allow families to focus on what matters most: quality time, meaningful connection, and peace of mind.

Advanced Home Watch Services is proud to stand as part of the solution—protecting homes, supporting families, and helping seniors thrive with dignity.

Patty's Special Offer

If you or someone you love is choosing to age in place and is seeking home watch, let me be the one to make sure the home stays in good repair.

Prevent problems upfront and provide peace of mind. Contact me for a free in-home estimate at https://advancedhomewatchservices.com/ or call 480-586-1098.

Empowering Choice in Healthcare with the Medical Health Inclusive Network with RxDirectCare and MDDPC

by Ray Vuono

Why Choice Matters More Than Ever

Healthcare is one of the most personal aspects of our lives, yet for many people and especially seniors, it feels like the least personal experience. Appointments are rushed, costs are unclear, and systems are confusing. Too often, people feel as though they have no real say in how their care is delivered.

The Medical Health Inclusive Network (MDHIN) was designed to change this reality. At its core, MDHIN is about giving people choice, the power to decide how, when, and where they receive care without being trapped by red tape or limited access.

Through its flagship programs, RxDirectCare and MDDPC (Medical Doctor Direct Primary Care), MDHIN introduces a new model of healthcare delivery that blends accessibility, affordability, and continuity. RxDirectCare offers concierge-style care through the pharmacy, bringing trusted, personalized healthcare directly into the community, while MDDPC provides affordable direct primary care that connects patients directly to physicians for continuous, relationship-based care.

Together, these programs form a comprehensive and inclusive network that makes healthcare simpler, more personal, and financially predictable. By giving patients the ability to choose between pharmacy-based or physician-based care or combine both within the same ecosystem, MDHIN empowers individuals and families to take control of their health journey with confidence and convenience.

The Challenges Seniors Face Today

Seniors often juggle:

- Multiple chronic conditions requiring ongoing monitoring.
- Medication management across several prescriptions.
- High out-of-pocket costs, even with Medicare.
- Limited access to local providers and long wait times.
- Confusion about billing and eligibility.

These challenges can make planning for long-term health feel overwhelming. RxDirectCare and MDDPC flips this equation by making access simpler, clearer, and more personal.

Concierge Care Through the Pharmacy

Pharmacies are one of the most trusted healthcare touchpoints. Seniors often see their pharmacist more frequently than their physician, and RxDirectCare builds on that trust by offering concierge-style healthcare directly through the pharmacy. Through this model, patients gain:

- Personalized consultations with pharmacists who know their health history.
- Streamlined access to collaborating physicians when advanced care is needed.
- Seamless services like PGx testing, preventive screenings, and care plan updates.
- More focused attention from pharmacy teams specifically equipped to serve RxDirectCare members.

This approach ensures that every visit feels more personal, intentional, and connected. It's not just picking up prescriptions—it's being cared for as a whole person.

Pharmacies that participate in RxDirectCare are designed to deliver concierge-level service, and because patients are part of the membership, pharmacists can dedicate more time and focus to consultations. Care is organized and documented, ensuring smooth communication with physicians. As a result, patients receive trusted advice and guidance without the delays of the traditional system.

Concierge care doesn't stop at the pharmacy counter. Through RxDirectCare, patients are also connected to collaborating medical doctors, either in person or virtually. This means seniors can get medical input faster, have their care plans coordinated between the pharmacy and the physician, and rely on a trusted, local team that understands their complete health picture.

In addition to RxDirectCare's pharmacy-driven concierge model, patients can also access MDDPC, Medical Doctor Direct Primary Care, a concierge program built around provider-led direct primary care. Together, these programs give patients flexible options to receive high-quality care where and how they need it most.For patients, the benefits are clear:

- **Direct Relationships with Providers:** MDDPC establishes a concierge-style, membership-based relationship directly with physicians, ensuring that patients receive continuous and personalized care rather than fragmented visits.
- **Ideal for High-Deductible Plans:** Patients with high insurance deductibles often delay care because of out-of-pocket costs. Both RxDirectCare and MDDPC memberships offer predictable, affordable monthly fees, helping patients manage their care without unexpected bills.
- **Improved Access:** For patients facing provider shortages or access issues, the combination of pharmacy-based and provider-based concierge care expands availability. Patients can see a pharmacist for routine needs or connect with a physician for more complex issues.
- **HSA Eligibility:** Both RxDirectCare and MDDPC programs are HSA-eligible, allowing patients to use pre-tax funds for membership fees, making the programs even more cost-effective.
- **Convenience & Continuity:** Whether through a local pharmacy or a direct physician relationship, patients gain streamlined access, care planning, and ongoing support. This dual model reduces unnecessary doctor visits, provides same-day access for many needs, and ensures better long-term engagement.

By offering RxDirectCare at the pharmacy and MDDPC with providers, patients are empowered with a concierge-level healthcare experience that works across settings, enhances access, and brings true value to those seeking affordable, dependable care outside of the traditional insurance model.

MDDPC and RxDirectCare: Complementary, Not Exclusive

Both MDDPC (Medical Doctor Direct Primary Care) and RxDirectCare (Pharmacy Concierge Care) are designed to work side by side. They are not exclusive to one provider type or one care setting. Instead, they can be used interchangeably or together, giving patients maximum flexibility and providers multiple ways to engage.

Both include:

- **Cross-Support:** A patient enrolled in MDDPC can still benefit from pharmacy encounters under RxDirectCare, and vice versa.
- **Shared Provider Network:** Both programs can utilize any participating provider group. Physicians, NPs, PAs, and pharmacists can all collaborate within the MDHIN and IPPN framework.
- **Patient Choice:** Some patients prefer a direct relationship with a physician, MDDPC. Others prefer pharmacy-based concierge care, RxDirectCare. Many will benefit from both, depending on the situation.
- **HSA-Eligible:** Both programs qualify for Health Savings Account (HSA) payments, giving patients an affordable way to manage care under either model.
- **Unified Ecosystem:** Together, MDDPC and RxDirect-Care create a comprehensive concierge care model. Providers deliver direct primary care through MDDPC, pharmacies

deliver accessible point-of-care services through RxDirectCare, and patients receive the convenience, affordability, and continuity they need.

MDDPC and RxDirectCare are two sides of the same coin—one provider-centric, one pharmacy-centric. They work independently, but integrate seamlessly under MDHIN, giving patients and providers true freedom of choice while expanding access to concierge care across the community.

This pharmacy-to-physician model ensures continuity and confidence in care.

Case Examples: A Senior's Experience

Take Mary, a seventy-two-year-old with diabetes and high blood pressure. She regularly visits her local pharmacy, where she joined RxDirectCare. Instead of waiting three months for her doctor's appointment, she can:

- Meet with her pharmacist for blood pressure and glucose checks.
- Receive concierge-style consultation about her medications.
- Use PGx testing to ensure her new prescription is right for her.
- Be connected directly to a collaborating physician when advanced care is needed.
- Have her care plan updated and shared across her care team.

For Mary, RxDirectCare means less waiting, more personalized attention, and true concierge care right in her own neighborhood.

John is a sixty-eight-year-old retiree managing both high blood pressure and cholesterol. Normally, he has to wait weeks for a doctor's appointment, then schedule a separate pharmacy trip to pick up his prescription. The back-and-forth leaves him frustrated, and sometimes he skips follow-up appointments because of the hassle.

After joining RxDirectCare, his experience looks very different.

One afternoon, John stops at his local pharmacy for his regular medication refill. As a member of RxDirectCare, the pharmacy team is equipped to do more than hand him his prescription. The pharmacist reviews his current medications, sees that an adjustment is needed, uses the collaborative practice agreement with a medical doctor, and within minutes, the physician electronically approves the change. John is able to receive his medication immediately and painlessly.

RxDirectCare is more than a program. It's a concierge care model delivered through local pharmacies to be accessible, transparent, and personalized. For seniors, it offers not just better healthcare, but better planning, confidence, and dignity. By putting pharmacies, patients, and providers at the center, RxDirectCare ensures that healthcare is not only about treating conditions, but about empowering people to live their best lives.

Ray's Special Offer

Discover how RxDirectCare, MDDPC, and MDHIN are redefining healthcare access through local pharmacies, provider networks, and membership-based care.

Visit: https://www.rxdirectcare.com/, https://www.mddpc.com/, and https://www.mdhin.com/ to learn more — and to find out how you can join today, submit this form: Interested to learn more about MDHIN and RxDirectCare.

Making the Move:

A Compassionate Guide to Selling Your Home

by Robert Cohen and Valerie Falkner

Deciding to sell a beloved home to downsize or move to a care facility can be one of life's most emotional and stressful transitions. Packing, selling cherished items, and relocating are challenging enough—especially when health, cognition, or mobility issues add complexity. Families must navigate not only the sale itself but also where to go next, and how to make a new space feel like home.

At Falkner Cohen Group, we specialize in helping clients and their families through these deeply personal moments. We have guided our own families through these decisions, combining our personal understanding with over forty years of real estate experience. Rob's legal background, our certifications as Senior Real Estate Specialists®, and our commitment to empathy give us a unique ability to support older adults and their families with confidence and care.

We hope this guide provides clarity, reassurance, and a sense of partnership as you begin exploring your next steps.

Valerie's Experience

I vividly remember the morning I got the call. My mom told me my dad had collapsed in cardiac arrest. Miraculously, it was right outside the hospital where he was headed for routine tests. After eleven minutes without a heartbeat, he survived and, against all odds, recovered. In the days that followed, our family had to confront a new reality: could my mom safely care for my dad at home?

Though my dad regained much of his strength, we faced changes: mobility challenges, new safety concerns, and daily tasks that became more difficult. Like many families, we had to weigh our options and talk openly about the future. Ultimately, my parents chose to remain in their home, and here's why: they live close to me—within a half-mile—and my sister and her husband (a firefighter) are nearby. We can respond quickly if help is needed. Their home, a single-level on a flat lot, already had many aging-friendly features: widened doorways, a spacious kitchen, and hard floors instead of carpet.

For now, moving doesn't make sense. Instead, we've made accessibility upgrades—grab bars, adjusted furniture, and smart devices for emergency calls. We've also explored reverse mortgage options to reduce financial stress and preserve independence.

Rob's Story: When the Time Comes to Move

Rob's experience unfolded differently. His mother developed dementia, and his father, a retired physician, wanted to care for her at home. For years, the family created a supportive environment that met their needs. But as his father's own health declined, it became clear that assisted living would offer better care and safety for both parents.

The transition was emotionally difficult, especially for a proud, independent man who wasn't used to asking for help. But ultimately, selling their home allowed them to fund quality care and stay together.

These personal experiences shape how we work with clients. We know how emotional these decisions can be, how long they can take, and how unique each situation is. Some families plan for years; others must act suddenly after an illness or injury. Either way, our approach is rooted in patience, respect, and compassion.

Our Philosophy: Guidance, Not Pressure

The decision to move should never feel rushed. We believe in starting the conversation early, sometimes years before a move actually happens. Our role is to serve as your resource, providing information, connecting you with trusted partners, and supporting you at your own pace.Every family's needs differ, but our guiding principle remains constant: we treat your family the way we'd want ours to be treated.

Legal and Ethical Considerations

When helping seniors sell a home—whether downsizing or aging in place—it's never just a transaction. It's a life-changing decision that requires expertise, ethics, and empathy.That's why we've pursued advanced training and certification as Senior Real Estate Specialists®. We understand not only the housing market, but also the legal, financial, and emotional nuances of late-in-life transitions.

Our Fiduciary Commitment

As licensed Realtors®, we're bound by fiduciary duty, meaning your interests always come first. We're not focused on a quick sale, but on your long-term well-being. That sometimes means encouraging you to slow down and consult with other professionals: elder law attorneys, financial planners, or care specialists. This extra guidance guarantees you can make fully informed decisions.

We ensure you understand every step and that all actions comply with current laws and ethical standards. Above all, your autonomy is paramount. You're in control, and we're here to provide guidance, options, and support—not pressure.

Navigating Cognitive or Health Concerns

One of the most sensitive areas we handle involves clients who may be experiencing cognitive decline. Real estate transactions require legal and mental capacity. We're trained to recognize warning signs such as confusion, poor judgment, or memory lapses, that could compromise a client's ability to make sound decisions.

If concerns arise, we pause the process and take the appropriate steps to protect the client, which may include:

- **Patience and clarity:** speaking in simple, clear terms and allowing extra time for questions.
- **Family involvement:** encouraging participation from trusted relatives, guardians, or legal advisors.
- **Professional evaluation:** when appropriate, referring for a competency assessment.
- **Documentation:** keeping detailed records of conversations and recommendations to ensure transparency and accountability.

Our goal is never to rush a sale, but to safeguard your well-being and rights.

Your Well-Being Is Our Bottom Line

We always recommend involving an elder law attorney early in the process. They ensure all documents are valid, protect your best interests, and confirm decisions are made freely and legally.We also encourage involving trusted family members or legal representatives so you have both emotional and practical support. This collaborative approach gives peace of mind to everyone involved.At the Falkner Cohen Group, we don't measure success by how fast a house sells, but by how supported and confident you feel throughout the process.

Our Senior-Centric Selling Process

Working with a Senior Real Estate Specialist® means every step of the process revolves around you: your comfort, your goals, and your pace. Our process is patient, transparent, and tailored.

Step 1: Initial Consultation

We begin with a home visit that includes you and any family members involved in decision-making. We'll:

- Listen to your concerns, needs, and goals.
- Walk through your home to understand its features and accessibility.
- Discuss the sales process and answer questions.
- Provide a Seller's Guide and a list of trusted partners to assist with downsizing, moving, and legal or financial planning.

This visit allows us to prepare a detailed plan for your home's preparation, pricing, and marketing strategy.

Step 2: Market Review and Planning

After researching market conditions and understanding your timeline, we schedule a second meeting to review our recommendations. We'll present:

- A written plan for decluttering, repairs, and optional upgrades.
- A comprehensive market analysis and suggested price range.
- Guidance on which improvements will have the greatest impact.

We encourage family participation in this step so everyone understands the plan and feels comfortable moving forward.

Some clients decide to move quickly, while others take months—or even years—to prepare. Either way, we remain your resource throughout, providing updated market information and answering questions as you evaluate your options.

Step 3: Listing and Marketing

Once you're ready, we finalize paperwork, set a timeline, and prepare your home for sale. Our team assists with every aspect: staging, photography, showings, and communication with potential buyers.We accompany showings upon request, provide written feedback, and keep you informed of market activity and offers. Transparency is key. You'll always know where things stand.

Step 4: Offers, Negotiation, and Closing

When offers arrive, we review each one carefully with you and your family. Our role is to ensure you understand your options and feel confident in your choices.

We manage all steps of the process, including:

- Negotiations and counteroffers.
- Buyer inspections and potential repairs.
- Title, escrow, and final documentation.
- Coordination with movers, estate sale planners, and other professionals.

Communication remains constant throughout via written summaries, regular updates, and in-person meetings as needed.

Our Team and Resources

Our "Dream Team" of senior-focused professionals includes:

- **Senior Transition Specialists:** Advisors who help evaluate care needs and future housing options.
- **Senior Move Managers:** Experts in downsizing, organizing, packing, and managing estate sales.

- **Elder Law Attorneys:** Professionals who guide legal matters like powers of attorney or trust documentation.
- **Financial Planners:** Advisors who analyze the financial implications of selling or aging in place.

We connect clients with these trusted partners to ensure every emotional, legal, and financial angle is considered.

Our Commitment to You

Selling a longtime home is rarely just a financial decision, it's a deeply personal transition. Our mission is to transform what can feel overwhelming into a thoughtful, empowering process.

We're committed to:

- **Patience:** Moving at your pace, not ours.
- **Compassion:** Recognizing the emotions tied to this life stage.
- **Communication:** Keeping you and your loved ones informed at every step.
- **Integrity:** Putting your best interests first, always.

We take pride in being not just real estate agents, but trusted advisors during one of life's most significant changes.

When we've done our job well, you don't just walk away with a sold home, you step into a new chapter that feels secure, supported, and hopeful.

Robert & Valerie's Special Offer

Deciding whether to sell your home or age in place can feel like an overwhelming task. A good place to start is by downloading our handout - 15 Crucial Questions to Ask Before Deciding to Age in Place. It provides all the most important details to consider so you can make the best decision for you and your family. Visit https://falkner-cohen-group.myflodesk.com/15-questions

Keeping Seniors Safe at Home

by Roland Ochoa

Have you ever wondered if there was an alternative to elderly care facilities that would allow your aging parent to stay in their own home and safely remain independent? At American Smart Homes, we strive to provide just that. We are one of the few—possibly the only—alarm companies in Scottsdale that focuses on helping the elderly.

As an adult child of an elderly parent myself, I understand the concerns you feel for your parent's safety and wellbeing as they age. This is why I feel passionate about offering security solutions that can bring you both peace of mind. We believe your loved one deserves to maintain their independence, comfort, and dignity at home for as long as they wish to. We help make this possible for them via a comprehensive security system that prioritizes their safety and individual wellness needs.

Too often, people's go-to for eldercare becomes assisted living out of frustration. However, if home security systems were marketed well, and made more easily available and affordable, our elders would be able to stay home. In many cases, families might not know how they can use their security system to ensure proper care and safety. This is where we come in.

How American Smart Homes Can Help

We help you assess what sensors and monitors would be the best fit to help your loved ones stay safe. Many people get alarm systems like the ones we offer to watch over their baby or pets, but rarely do they utilize them for effective home safety alerts, to keep energy costs down, or to care for elderly parents. I didn't even consider our alarm systems for these solutions until I began hearing concerning stories online and on the radio about elder care in facilities gone wrong. This highlighted how much seniors could benefit from a well-designed alarm and monitoring system.

At American Smart Homes, we pride ourselves on being a local, faith-based, small business deeply committed to helping elders stay safe and independent at home. We provide security alarms, cameras, life safety, flood control, automation installation, and monitoring services to homes and small businesses in Phoenix, Arizona, and surrounding areas such as Glendale, Peoria, Waddell, Litchfield Park, Avondale, Goodyear, Anthem, Carefree, Cave Creek, Scottsdale, Paradise Valley, Fountain Hills, and beyond.

We install smart home security, monitoring, and automation systems for elders that their loved ones can access and rely on remotely. This helps ensure that your loved one will be okay without you needing to be there 24/7. Our services include:

- **Wellness monitoring** (mutually agreed upon indoor cameras as well as motion-tracking sensors).
- **Wearable medical pendants** (so your parent can alert someone if they don't feel safe).

- **Safety sensors to help monitor medicine intake,** water leaks, gas burners, smoke detectors, and carbon monoxide detectors.
- **Alarms and remote controls** (arm/disarm alarms, check if door is locked, see if windows or doors are open, adjust thermostat, control lights, open/close garage door/s).
- **Incident response** so that if smoke, flood, or gas leaks occur you are alerted and can view a live feed as well as unlock the door from afar for emergency responders to enter, turn off the water main, etc.
- **Support for elders with dementia** and/or a tendency to wander (alerts for unexpected motion, doors being opened, or their being out of bed too long or too little).

If break-ins are a concern, there are also gun motion sensors and gunshot detectors. You can even run sprinklers and monitor solar with our systems. All of this comes with an app/web access, so you can see what's going on, even from out of town. Our systems help you monitor your parents, and respond when necessary, without being overbearing. If your loved one is still walking, talking, and able to live at home, these tools help you—and them—keep things that way for as long as possible!

Your Loved Ones' Needs Come First

As the owner of American Smart Homes, my service recommendations are informed by a wealth of experience. I've worked for Brinks, ADT, Alert 360, and AAA. In those jobs, the salespeople are often urged to sell customers things they don't need, but in our company, I strive to reconnect that missing link between sales and what the customer actually needs. To ensure success for my customers, I respond accordingly to each person's situation and only offer specifically relevant recommendations. I always come out and do a walkthrough first, so there's no disconnect between what the customer needs and what I'm recommending.

My personal and business mission is to help our local seniors stay safe. I know the Phoenix area well. I've lived in the valley since 1983. I come from a military family: my grandfather did tours in WWII and the Korean War, my dad did three tours in Vietnam, and my niece and nephew now serve. I graduated from Trevor Browne High School, and I have been in the special systems industry since 1999.

With an IT background, I consider myself one of the more knowledgeable techs in the valley, especially when it comes to working with cameras and wifi related products (due to the work I did with Cox and Vonage Business). Over time, I've learned that when there are issues, it's almost never the camera that prolongs repairs; it's the tech. As a result, I've built up my skills so that I can now diagnose and treat almost any issue with network-related products in a matter of minutes, not hours!

If you're considering how best to support your loved one(s) continuing their life at home, I suggest first opening up a conversation with them about their fears, concerns, and what they need in order to remain independent. Ask questions like:

- What sensors alert you when something unusual happens?
- What happens in an emergency?
- Who responds?
- What changes would you make you feel safer in your home?

Then, if there's a desire for safety and security, you can schedule a walkthrough with us at no charge. We can help you assess your situation, and look for anything potentially hazardous or anything that may cause difficulty—old plumbing (flood risk), gas stove, doors that are hard to lock, etc. *Please note*: We only schedule one appointment per day to ensure we can take our time with each individual customer to fully understand their needs. We will never have the need to "get to our next appointment."

How We Build Your Security Package for Optimum Safety

When building your security package, it's good to start with the core safety concerns, such as smoke, carbon monoxide, and fall detection, a medical pendant, and a wellness-cam. Then, if necessary, we can build out your system to add on features like light and thermostat monitors, as well as remote controls. I encourage families to see it as a system you build over time, as your loved one's needs may change.

The added automation systems are often wants, not needs. However, door-lock automation *can* be a need; it is definitely more convenient and safer than putting a key in a fake rock. The garage door opener automation is a favorite. Thermostat and lighting automation are not necessities, but nice to have as they can help keep utility costs down, especially with all the data centers going up and prices skyrocketing.

With daily monitoring or security, it's essential to establish trust and a routine with your parent(s) or loved ones who you are helping. We install, test, and educate everyone who needs to know about the new security system. Repetition of what you've learned, or how to run the system, is necessary to ensure comprehension of the system as with any new technology.

All technology and electronics will likely increase in cost over time, so I recommend putting the pieces you need in place now. The needs and costs will depend on the home. For example, when has your home been plumbed last? If it's old, I recommend putting water sensors in. I've lived through a flood before; it can take weeks to get it fully cleaned up and the area livable again!

If your loved one is a heavy sleeper, smoke detectors with loud alerts that also communicate with first responders are essential. If the detectors only alert those in the home, no one else would know the house is on fire, unless it's linked to the monitoring system. This is also true with carbon monoxide detectors.

I also strongly suggest a basic motion sensor that alerts the authorities in case of break-ins. The security panel does take a snapshot of anyone trying to disarm the system, and when it's live in the alarm state, it records a video. The monitoring station can speak to anyone through the alarm panel (if applicable) to verify a false alarm and cancel first responder dispatch if necessary. This helps keep costs down for the consumer.

The Difference Service, Integrity, and Freedom Make

For elders on fixed incomes, we have a base system package that is cost-efficient, which can be built upon gradually as more security or monitoring devices are needed. We also give free medical pendants to customers who are fifty-five or older when they purchase any system with us. The pendants only work at home because you have to be connected to the system, but there is a more mobile one in the works that will be GPS-oriented. Everything connected to our system is currently local, but a service called Dash will be able to alert the system through monitoring and use GPS to locate where your loved ones are, in order to dispatch first responders to their exact location.

Our slogan is: Service, Integrity, Freedom. We don't require our customers to do contracts. You can come and go as you please. Our monthly service fee is one of the lowest for a full-service company. And the installation fee is waived for the local elderly community.

If you work with us, you'll get a system built to suit your parent's situation. Rather than a one-size-fits-all system, we provide a walkthrough to better understand the layout, routine, and risks; providing recommendations you can scale over time, starting with what matters most now. You'll receive responsive maintenance service from our knowledgeable technicians; and a partner to help make sure your loved one is able to stay at home safely, comfortably, and with dignity.

How Working with an Elder Law Attorney Helps Families Achieve the Best Outcomes

by Stephanie Bivens

Aging brings both joys and challenges. Families often find themselves navigating complicated legal, medical, and financial systems while trying to honor their loved one's wishes and maintain peace at home. In these moments, an elder law attorney can make all the difference. Elder law attorneys focus on the intersection of law, aging, and caregiving. We don't just prepare documents—we prepare families for the road ahead.

Estate Planning: Building a Foundation for Security and Clarity

For many families, estate planning is the first step toward peace of mind. A skilled elder law attorney looks at the whole picture: your health, family dynamics, goals, finances, and potential care needs, to create a plan that works for you today and adapts for tomorrow.

An estate plan is not just one document; it's a coordinated set of legal tools designed to address incapacity, legacy, and probate avoidance. Without a proper plan, families often face uncertainty, added legal costs, conflict, and outcomes they never intended.So, what should every person have in place?

The Basic Documents for Everyone

- **Durable Financial Power of Attorney:** Authorizes someone to manage your finances if you are unable to do so.
- **Medical Directives (Health Care and Mental Health Care Power of Attorney, Living Will, and HIPAA Release):** Clarify your medical wishes, designate decision-makers, and ensure healthcare providers can share vital information with those you choose.
- **Last Will and/or Revocable Trust:** Provides clear instructions on who will manage your estate and how your assets will be distributed.

Client Story: The Reynolds Family

When Mrs. Reynolds, age seventy-two, came to us, she had three adult children with very different circumstances: the eldest was financially responsible, the middle child was struggling with debt, and the youngest had special needs. She feared that leaving an inheritance outright might cause more harm than good. We created a trust that protected Mrs. Reynolds' estate, managed the middle child's inheritance responsibly, and set up a third-party special needs trust for her youngest child, so she could both inherit and keep her public benefits.

Years later, when Mrs. Reynolds passed, her children found comfort knowing their mother's wishes were clear. Instead of probate or family disputes, they were able to grieve and support one another.

Client Story:
Dave and Cindy

When Dave and Cindy visited our office, Dave had just been diagnosed with early-stage dementia. As the primary manager of their finances, Dave worried about the future. We developed a comprehensive estate plan.As Dave's condition progressed, Cindy seamlessly stepped into her role as sole trustee and decision-maker—because the documents were already in place.

Years later, she shared:"Every time a bank asks for Dave's power of attorney or a doctor asks for his medical directives, I'm grateful we worked with you. Having the right documents has made it so much easier to take care of Dave and our finances. When I hear the struggles of families without these protections, I realize how much heartache we've avoided. Thank you."Today, as Dave receives memory care and hospice support, Cindy knows we'll be there for her again when the time comes.

Probate Avoidance:
Keeping Your Family Out of Court

Most people know they want to avoid probate, even if they aren't exactly sure what it is. Probate is a court-supervised process where a judge appoints a Personal Representative to administer a deceased person's estate.

Spoiler alert: having a Will does not avoid probate. Whether probate is required depends on how the decedent's assets were titled at death, and their value. In Arizona, probate is necessary if: Real estate titled in the decedent's name has more than $300,000 in equity, or other assets, such as bank accounts, cars, or brokerage accounts, exceed $200,000 in value. Keep in mind: "estate" assets are those owned solely by the decedent, not those that pass automatically through a trust, joint ownership, or beneficiary designation.

Spoiler alert number two: Adding your child to your deed or making them a joint owner on your accounts to "avoid probate" is generally not advised. This can cause unfavorable capital gains tax issues for your child and create liability risks for you.

The good news? Probate can be avoided with proper estate planning that reflects your wishes.

Reasons to Avoid Probate

- **Privacy:** Probate is public. Anyone can access details of your estate.
- **Cost Savings:** Court and attorney fees reduce the estate's value.
- **Time Savings:** Probate can take months, or even years.
- **Less Burden on Family:** Streamlined transfers mean less stress and court involvement for your loved ones during a difficult time.

Long-Term Care Asset Protection Planning: Balancing Care and Preservation

Few families are prepared for the financial shock of long-term care. Home care, assisted living, memory care, and nursing home costs can drain a lifetime of savings in just a few years. *Note*: Medicare does not cover these expenses.

Elder law attorneys help families understand the *real costs* of long-term care, analyze their options, and implement strategies that protect assets, preserve dignity, and provide peace of mind.

When it comes to paying for long-term care, there are only three options:

- **Private Pay:** using your own income and savings.
- **Long-Term Care Insurance:** if you planned ahead and invested in a policy.
- **Public Benefits:** such as Veterans Aid & Attendance or Medicaid, known in Arizona as the Arizona Long Term Care System (ALTCS).

Imagine your spouse or parent suffers from a stroke and needs assistance with daily activities. Depending on the level of care, costs can run from $5,000 to $15,000 per month. For most families, this isn't sustainable, and the financial strain quickly adds emotional stress to an already difficult situation.

Client Story: The Lopez Family

Carlos and Elena Lopez worked hard and saved for retirement. But when Carlos was diagnosed with Parkinson's disease, Elena realized she could no longer provide the care he needed at home. The cost of assisted living threatened to wipe out their savings, leaving her with nothing to live on. Working together, we designed a Medicaid planning strategy that allowed Carlos to qualify for ALTCS benefits while preserving 95 percent of their assets for Elena's future. Instead of losing everything, Elena remained financially secure, and Carlos received the care he needed.

Client Story: Charles and Gary

Charles, age sixty, worried that his father's care costs would destroy his own retirement plans. Gary, age eighty-five, had already been in memory care for three years and only had six months of funds left. We obtained ALTCS approval, moving Gary seamlessly from private pay to ALTCS pay. The result: Gary received uninterrupted care, and Charles gained peace of mind knowing his father's needs were met without sacrificing his own retirement security.

Medicaid (Arizona Long Term Care System – ALTCS) Myths

- **"I have too much to qualify for ALTCS."**

  Maybe . . . but maybe not. With proper planning, you can keep more than you think.

- **"The state will take my house."**

  With the right strategies, your home can be protected from liens and estate recovery.

- **"The social worker will handle it for me."**

  They may help with the application, but they are not experts in asset protection or the law.

- **"I can apply on my own."**

  You can, but just like representing yourself in court, it may not lead to the best outcome.

Guardianship and Conservatorship: Protecting Loved Ones When Capacity Declines

Sometimes a loved one reaches a point where they can no longer manage their affairs. Cognitive decline, dementia, or sudden illness can leave families scrambling to protect them. In some cases, guardianship or conservatorship may be necessary.

Client Story: Two Sisters

Two sisters, Emily and Rachel, were in conflict over their mother's care. Their mother, Eleanor, had advanced dementia and no powers of attorney in place. One daughter believed Eleanor should move to a memory care facility, while the other wanted to keep her at home. Without powers of attorney, the daughters had equal authority for medical decision making and neither had legal authority to handle finances. We petitioned the court for guardianship and conservatorship, ultimately appointing Rachel, while also establishing safeguards so Emily had transparency and input. This legal framework eased tensions, gave their mother the care she needed, and reduced the bitter disputes that threatened to tear the family apart.

Client Story: Protecting a Father with Lewy Body Dementia

When John's family came to us, he had been diagnosed with Lewy Body Dementia and was experiencing serious behavioral changes. Once independent and strong-willed, John refused essential medical care and resisted the in-home assistance he desperately needed. His choices, while made in confusion, were putting his health and safety at risk. We guided John's family through the guardianship process. This allowed his daughter to make the proper medical decisions he could no longer make for himself. The result:

John received consistent care, his health stabilized, and he remained safe and supported.

Steps to Take if a Loved One Shows Signs of Declining Capacity

- Start with a medical evaluation to rule out treatable causes.
- Look for existing estate planning documents.
- Consult an elder law attorney to review existing estate planning documents—or to create new ones—and to discuss whether guardianship or conservatorship may be necessary.
- Keep communication open with family to reduce conflict.

Planning early always leads to better outcomes. If a loved one is diagnosed with a chronic illness, their caregiving responsibilities are increasing, or there is a concern about protecting your family home or savings, start now.

The Ripple Effect: Benefits Beyond the Legal Documents

Working with an elder law attorney goes beyond drafting documents, applying for Medicaid long term care benefits, or the courtroom. Families gain peace of mind, clarity, and relief from the overwhelming uncertainty they are faced with. Caregivers can focus on their relationships rather than endless problem-solving. Ultimately, the work we do strengthens families. Elder law attorneys are not simply legal professionals—we are guides, advocates, and partners in one of life's most challenging seasons. That is the true value of elder law.

Stephanie's Special Offer

Take the Next Step

You don't have to navigate these challenges alone. The right legal guidance can make all the difference for you and your loved ones. To see how we can help, call Bivens & Associates, PLLC today at 480-922-1010 or email Info@bivenslaw.com to schedule your consultation with one of our experienced attorneys. Let us put our knowledge and compassion to work for you.

The Benefits of Reverse Mortgages

by Suzanne Soderberg

In the simplest of terms, a reverse mortgage is a financial tool that gives homeowners the ability to convert the equity in their house into cash. It's been wrongly believed that reverse mortgages are bad, and only what desperate people do when they think they are about to lose their home, as a last resort. There are assumptions that they are just for house rich, cash poor seniors, when no other options are available to them.

Believe it or not, there are many situations where a reverse mortgage would make sense. They aren't for everyone, but in the right situation, they are a great option. There has been too much negative press and misinformation floating around for far too long, keeping those that could benefit from them scared and unsure about applying for one.

There are several scenarios where a reverse mortgage could make sense for someone.

Eliminate Your Mandatory Monthly Mortgage Payment

One scenario could help eliminate your mandatory monthly mortgage payment. This is the most widely used benefit of a reverse mortgage. With a reverse mortgage, you are no longer required to make your monthly mortgage payment; however, you can make the payment should you choose to. Imagine what retirement would be like without having to make a monthly mortgage payment.

If you are still in the workforce, you could redirect that payment to your savings account and build it up for when you retire. If you are already retired, you can reduce the amount of money you have to take from your savings or retirement account every month for everyday living expenses.

Many people think that they no longer own their home when they do a reverse mortgage. That is simply not true. You always retain ownership of your home. It is the same as if you had a traditional mortgage. Reverse and traditional mortgages have very similar rules and characteristics.

Both mortgages use the home as collateral. You still have ownership rights, and your heirs will still inherit your home should you wish to pass it on to them. Since there is no mandatory monthly mortgage payment, you must pay your property taxes, insurance, and any association dues associated with the home, and you must keep the home in good condition.

Age in Place

In another scenario, a reverse mortgage can be a valuable financial solution for older homeowners who want to age in place with comfort, dignity, and independence. This loan allows individuals sixty-two and older to convert a portion of their home equity into tax-free funds, without selling their home or taking on monthly mortgage payments.

The money can be used to pay for in-home care services, medical expenses, daily living costs, or even essential home modifications like stair lifts, walk-in tubs, or wheelchair-accessible entryways. Just think of being able to modify the home you've lived in for most of your adult life so you can remain in it, be comfortable, and age in place safely and securely.

For many, it provides peace of mind that comes with staying in familiar surroundings while having the financial flexibility to maintain their lifestyle and address changing needs. Since the homeowner retains full ownership of the home, and repayment is typically deferred until the home is sold or the borrower leaves the residence, it offers both stability and security during retirement. Used strategically, a reverse mortgage can help create a sustainable plan for aging in place, on your own terms.

Guarantee Your Spouse Can Remain in the Home

Obtaining a reverse mortgage can also be used to guarantee your spouse will remain in the home after you have passed. For many retirees, nothing is more important than preserving their independence and protecting their loved ones from added stress. The thought of becoming a burden to their children weighs heavily, often just as much as financial concerns. Most seniors dream of spending their later years in their home filled with memories, not in someone else's spare room or a facility that doesn't feel like their own. Aging in place is about more than staying put, it's about staying YOU.

If a reverse mortgage borrower passes away, federal protections allow an eligible non-borrowing spouse (typically the surviving spouse who wasn't listed as a borrower on the loan) to remain in the home as long as certain conditions are met. The surviving spouse must have been married to the borrower at the time of the loan's closing. The loan must be an FHA-insured Home Equity Conversion Mortgage. They must continue to meet loan obligations like paying property taxes, homeowners' insurance, HOA fees and maintaining the home. As long as all of these things are true, they can remain living in the home as their primary residence and do not have to repay the loan. This protection helps ensure that a surviving spouse isn't forced out of the home during an already difficult time.

Access Income in Retirement

A reverse mortgage gives you the opportunity to access the equity in your home in several different ways. You can receive the equity as

1. A lump sum
2. Monthly tenured payment for as long as you live in the home
3. A line of credit
4. Specified monthly amount for a certain amount of time
5. Any combination of one, two, and three.

This money is received as tax-free income, since it is your equity you are accessing. If you need $20,000, you withdraw $20,000. Imagine accessing money from your equity instead of withdrawing it from your retirement accounts and depleting the principal you have. In addition, it doesn't affect the calculation of how much of your social security is taxable, nor is it counted in the calculation that determines your Medicare premium.

Living Out Your Bucket List

Did you ever create a bucket list of things you wanted to do before you left this earth? It's probably safe to say some of the things on that list were not checked off because you didn't have the money to pay for them.

Many retired couples want to travel the world, go on a cruise, or spend more time making memories with their children and grandchildren. However, the fear of running out of money, or wanting to leave their equity to their heirs, keeps them from doing the things they want to do in their retirement.

Instead of living out their bucket list of items, they live on the fear of hoarding all of the equity for those "just in case" and "what if" we need the money later. Meanwhile, they have the house they've lived in for decades that holds a goldmine of equity. A reverse mortgage can provide you with the money you need to start living your life and checking off those bucket list items. All without a mortgage payment or having to liquidate your brokerage accounts or 401Ks that are there to get you through retirement.

Eliminate Credit Card Debt

A reverse mortgage gives you access to the equity in your home to help pay off credit card debt or even auto loans. Much of the retiring population goes into retirement with a lot of credit card debt. Paying off these monthly payments gives you increased cash flow into the household.

Imagine paying off a credit card with a 22 percent APR rate and its required monthly minimum payment. What would that do for your peace of mind? Those payments can be overwhelming when you are living on a fixed income.

You can use the reverse mortgage to give you access to the equity in the home to help pay off auto loans, installment loans, medical bills, and even collection accounts. You can breathe a sigh of relief knowing you do not have those monthly payments or a monthly mortgage payment to pay.

In the end, a reverse mortgage is a highly beneficial tool that can be used to set seniors up for a peaceful, abundant, and worry-free life.

Suzanne's Special Offer

If you are interested in hearing more about how a Reverse Mortgage might work for your situation, please reach out to me via email at Suzanne@suzannesoderberg.com for a no obligation consultation.

What's Next?

As we turn the final page of this anthology, our mission extends far beyond these words. Each story, insight, and resource shared throughout this collection has one unifying purpose—to help families navigate the often-overwhelming journey of senior care with confidence, compassion, and clarity. Whether you're just beginning to explore care options for a loved one or are deep in the process of coordinating support, you are not alone.

The professionals featured in this book—financial planners, home health providers, legal experts, and insurance specialists—represent more than individual services; together, they form a network of advocates devoted to empowering families through every stage of aging care. Their collective experience ensures that every decision made is grounded in both practicality and heart.

But this is only the beginning. Our next chapter is one of connection—linking families with trusted resources, expanding educational outreach, and continuing the conversation about how we can best honor our elders with dignity and grace. We invite you to reach out, ask questions, and engage with the contributors whose passion has shaped these pages.

The future of senior care depends on collaboration and awareness. By sharing what we've learned and standing together as a community of caregivers, professionals, and families, we can build a future where aging is embraced with understanding, respect, and unwavering support. Together, we're redefining what it means to care—one story, one resource, and one family at a time.

About the Authors

Angela Garrett

Angela Garrett is the Director of Operations of Prime IV Hydration and Wellness in Scottsdale. She has spent the past 13 years managing and working day to day in a successful growing lab testing franchise.

That grew to her passion for health and wellness. Angela loves being in the day-to-day operations helping to grow and excel the brand of Prime IV Hydration and Wellness. She has an exceptional medical staff and team whose main focus is safety and giving each client a spa-like experience while getting hydration with tailored vitamins, minerals and nutrients. She says, "Our mission is to deliver vitamins, nutrients, aminos, peptides and NAD+ through IV infusion and Intramuscular injections, to create a cutting-edge health and wellness experience, so that people live, feel and perform better".

Angela takes accountability for the success of her franchise, and she proactively makes needed adjustments to achieve results.

In her free time, she loves spending time with her family. She and her husband Robert have 2 girls that keeps them on the go outside of work.

Angela Garrett

Angela Garrett is the Director of Operations at Any Lab Test Now, a leader in direct-access lab testing services across the United States. With over 13 years of experience managing lab testing franchises, Angela has developed a deep passion for health and wellness. Her focus lies in ensuring that the services offered are accessible, convenient, and accommodating to all demographics, including the elderly.]

Angela is instrumental in the day-to-day operations, helping Any Lab Test Now provide efficient, confidential, and affordable testing services. She ensures that specialized services like TB skin tests, UTI checks, PT INR checks, and annual check-up panels are readily available and easily accessible for elderly clients and others who might benefit from preventive care.

Angela's role and leadership align perfectly with Any Lab Test Now's mission to empower individuals to take control of their health with ease, convenience, and transparency. Outside of her professional life, Angela enjoys spending time with her family, staying active with her husband Robert and their two daughters.

Cameron Svendsen

Cameron Svendsen is a licensed clinical social worker, speaker, and author with over 25 years in the healthcare industry. Cameron co-founded Palliative Care Alliance, a trailblazing community-based program that provides clinical support to patients with chronic and serious illnesses. He's also played a pivotal role in the significant growth and reputation of Faith Hospice in Phoenix. Currently, Cameron leverages his expertise as the Chief Strategy Officer for a select group of innovative healthcare companies across the valley.

Cedric Wade

Cedric Wade spent over 30 years helping individuals achieve their financial goals, which ultimately led him to discover his true passion—supporting seniors during major life transitions. In June 2019, Cedric launched Caring Transitions of Scottsdale, a franchise dedicated to assisting seniors with downsizing, relocating, and estate liquidation.

Cedric specializes in managing online estate sales, enabling clients to efficiently liquidate the entire contents of their homes—typically within a two- to three-week timeframe. Beyond estate sales, he provides comprehensive move management services, including:

- Packing and unpacking assistance
- Coordination of all aspects of the move

Recognizing that relocation can be one of life's most stressful events, Cedric offers a stress-free, one-stop solution that handles the entire process from start to finish—with compassion, professionalism, and care.

Doug Sparks

Doug Sparks is the Founder and CEO of Precision Value Based Management. Doug is a currently recognized healthcare strategist with over 38 years of experience in the industry following eight successful years on Wall Street. He founded Precision Value Based Management with the passion to address the coming needs of value-based compliance mandates.

In the past he served as the Chairman of a publicly traded physical therapy company, accelerating revenues, and taking them through a completed acquisition. Following this Since 2002, he has built comprehensive compliance and revenue models for physicians, groups, hospitals, ACOs, IPAs among other various health care industry stakeholders.

Dr. Molly Powiada

Dr. Molly Powiada, Owner of Fortitude Performance Chiropractic, is a Doctor of Chiropractic passionate about helping seniors stay strong, mobile, and independent. Through evidence based, individualized programs, she helps prevent falls, surgeries, and hospitalizations so later decades are not marked by decline but filled with family, travel, and the activities they love. Dr. Molly's mission is to help people not just live longer but truly live well

David Endre

David Endre is dedicated to helping seniors live safely and purposefully at home. With more than 20 years of experience building continuous improvement cultures, he brought his passion for people into senior care through Home Matters Caregiving in Scottsdale. His focus is on helping families find peace of mind while supporting seniors in maintaining independence and the daily routines that bring comfort and joy.

John Jeffery

John Jeffery and his wife Lynda Carter, started Jeffery Insurance Agency 15 years ago as Medicare agents. John spent 5 years working with ALTCS provider: Bridgeway Health Solutions in charge of Medicare sales for the state of Arizona. Lynda has over 30 years Medicare and facility experience. With over 14 years with United Healthcare as an account manager for Optum. Together, they are Arizona's senior healthcare resource

Kendra Seavey

Kendra Seavey is President and CEO of care.coach, leading innovations that help older adults live safely and independently at home. With over 15 years in aging services, healthcare, and digital health, she brings experience across providers, payers, and technology. Kendra combines deep expertise with empathy to empower families and seniors, shaping the future of aging with human-centered solutions.

Malea Madrid

I began my career in banking at 17, later working in construction HR, international finance, and accounting before serving seniors in Sun City. I saw firsthand how overwhelming taxes and paperwork can be, and how easily scams take hold. Drawing from my professional background and caring for my grandparents, I founded Consider It Done Seniors and Golden Rule Alliance – dedicated to simplifying paperwork, protecting seniors from fraud, and ensuring their voices are respected.

Marcus Moran

Marcus Moran is a graduate from the University of Utah. Prior to becoming a licensed insurance professional in 2013, Marcus spent 7 years helping seniors with navigating the Assisted Living Decision. Marcus gained practical experience with the inner workings of both Medicare and Long-Term Care, This experience proved invaluable creating an awareness of how Medicare and Long-Term Care decisions affect the lives of both the insured and their families.

Patty Knox-Hermann

I began as a financial advisor and then followed my calling into Real Estate by starting my brokerage, Block Party Realty, where I throw a community block party with every listing! My professional reach expanded with Advanced Home Watch Services, LLC. I provide trusted weekly checks and concierge services for Seniors aging in place, helping them maintain two of their most valuable assets, their home and their independence.

Ray Vuono

Ray Vuono is the CEO and founder of several healthcare ventures, including RxDirectCare, Medical Doctor Direct Primary Care (MDDPC), Independent Pharmacy Provider Network (IPPN), Connect Health Information Network (ConnectHIN), and MD Health Inclusive Network (MDHIN). His work focuses on empowering pharmacies and providers to deliver accessible, affordable care through innovative membership programs and collaborative networks. With a background in technology and patient engagement, Ray's mission is to give people greater choice, convenience, and dignity in planning and receiving their healthcare.

Robert Cohen & Valerie Falkner

The Falkner Cohen Group (FCG), an eXp Luxury authority led by Valerie Falkner and Robert Cohen, specializes in Scottsdale luxury real estate. With over $500 million in Arizona sales and 40+ years of combined experience, FCG expertly assists diverse clients, from investors to second-home owners. We are passionate, however, about serving seniors, holding the SRES certification. We provide strategic, empathetic guidance for major decisions like downsizing and aging in place.

Roland Ochoa

When it comes to home security and automation, American Smart Homes stands out as a trusted provider in the Phoenix Metropolitan area. American Smart Homes has been offering peace of mind and convenience to homeowners through state-of-the-art alarm systems, cameras, life safety, flood control, and automation solutions.

Our systems provide so many benefits that we now refer to them as a Whole Home Management System! They provide as a burglar deterrent, a way to put eyes on our homes while away, be notified of gas leaks, fire, flooding, a way to operate your homes doors, lighting, energy and to care for the disabled, our pets and elderly. We would love to be a part of your life in helping secure your home with great understanding and support.

Service. Integrity. Freedom.

Stephanie Bivens

Stephanie Bivens, Esq., CELA* is a distinguished attorney, author and speaker with extensive experience in estate planning, probate, elder law, and special needs planning. Bivens & Associates PLLC is one of Arizona's leading estate/trust and elder law firms, known for legal expertise and commitment to excellence. Ms. Bivens and her firm have advised and represented thousands of clients for over 25 years.

*Certified Elder Law Attorney, by National Elder Law Foundation

Stephanie Russell, BSN, RN

Stephanie Russell, RN, BSN, is a compassionate advocate for seniors and their families. Her deep understanding of the challenges faced by aging individuals and their caregivers inspired her to launch Concierge Senior Care Management and write Planned Senior Moments, a practical guide aimed at helping families navigate the intricacies of senior care with confidence and foresight.

Suzanne Söderberg

Suzanne Söderberg helps homeowners 62+ unlock home equity with reverse mortgages to fund retirement, care needs, or simply enjoy life with more financial freedom. Partnering with financial professionals, in-home care providers, and Aging in Place Specialists, she offers education, integrity, and tailored solutions that preserve independence while enhancing long-term plans. With over 25 years of experience, Suzanne empowers seniors to stay in the homes they love while securing peace of mind.

Interested in Being an Author in an Upcoming Book?

Are you interested in sharing your experience with fellow senior care specialists from a variety of fields? Planned Senior Moments is just the beginning of our journey.

Upcoming editions are planned for:

- Phoenix
- Chandler
- Sun City
- Cave Creek

If you would like to schedule a call to learn more about becoming an author in future editions, please visit SeniorCareofAZ.com/plannedseniormoments and learn more about Planned Senior Moments.

Made in the USA
Coppell, TX
11 February 2026